MW01258168

The D..... ...ontemporary African So...

Bibiana M. Ngundo

The Diviner in contemporary African Society

Case of the Akamba Christians of Machakos, Kenya

LAP LAMBERT Academic Publishing

Impressum / Imprint

Bibliografische Information der Deutschen Nationalbibliothek: Die Deutsche Nationalbibliothek verzeichnet diese Publikation in der Deutschen Nationalbibliografie; detaillierte bibliografische Daten sind im Internet über http://dnb.d-nb.de abrufbar.

Bibliographic information published by the Deutsche Nationalbibliothek: The Deutsche Nationalbibliothek lists this publication in the Deutsche Nationalbibliografie; detailed bibliographic data are available in the Internet at http://dnb.d-nb.de.

Coverbild / Cover image: www.ingimage.com

Verlag / Publisher:
LAP LAMBERT Academic Publishing
ist ein Imprint der / is a trademark of
AV Akademikerverlag GmbH & Co. KG
Heinrich-Böcking-Str. 6-8, 66121 Saarbrücken, Deutschland / Germany
Email: info@lap-publishing.com

Herstellung: siehe letzte Seite /
Printed at: see last page
ISBN: 978-3-8383-5451-4

Contents

CHAPTER ONE: GENERAL INTRODUCTION

Background information

The Catholic Diocese of Machakos covers an area of 15,183 sq. km. The inhabitants of Kamba land are mainly the Akamba people found in three counties namely; Machakos County, Makueni County and Kitui County. Machakos county has eight districts and thirty eighty wards in total. The language of the Akamba is *kikamba*. Machakos Diocese was curved from Nairobi Archdiocese in 1969 and Bishop Raphael Ndingi Mwana'a Nzeki was appointed its first Bishop. In 1971 he was transferred to Nakuru Diocese. He moved from Machakos in 1973. Late Bishop Urbanus Kioko assumed shepherd-ship of Machakos Diocese the same year. On 15th March, 2003 Bishop Kioko resigned and Rev. Fr. Martin Kivuva Musonde was consecrated on 3rd June 2003 as the Bishop of the Catholic Diocese of Machakos.

The Diocese has grown tremendously over the past 32 years. By June 2006, the Diocese had a Catholic population of 781, 799 covering 52 parishes with 9 Deaneries, 134 Diocesan priests, 134 senior seminarians, 1,346 primary schools, 252 Secondary Schools, 30 Polytechnics, 585 Nursery schools, 601 full time Catechists, 367 volunteer Catechists, 2 Hospitals and 22 Dispensaries (The Kenya Catholic Secretariat, 2006).

The Catholic Diocese of Machakos has taken to heart the words of Our Lord Jesus Christ found in the Gospel of John 17: 18-21, "that all may be one" as the motto of the clergy, the religious and all the people of God. The Diocese evangelizes through Schools, Small Christian Communities, care of the poor, the sick and the aged among other ways.

The research problem of this study is rooted in the researcher's personal observation of the Akamba people's behavior in relation to diviners. The researcher has observed that despite the hard work of evangelization, traditional religion and culture have continued to affect people in one way or another. The environment with its spiritual and material components dictate the way the Akamba view themselves as a people and how they relate with and to each other, and with the universe as a whole. Thus, the beliefs that people have, are born out of this interaction. Mbula (1982:40) observes that, traditional African beliefs are based on the individual's self awareness, his relationship with others and with the physical and spiritual world around him. She summarizes the Mukamba's way of life into a single "creed" as follows:

> I am an absolute Mukamba (Mukamba kivindyo), who knows and
> believes in the purity of rituals, and I know that these rites can bring
> forth life. I know the things that can cause misfortune, and I offer
> sacrifice to God for rain to fall. To be sure that I am an absolute
> Mukamba, I believe that a barren woman, when treated with
> purifying ritual medicine (emutonye ng'ondu), will bring forth
> offspring. I know right from wrong (na wisi maundu ala me
> muisyo), and know that worshiping God (Ngai) restores blessings to
> man and woman (Mbula, 1982: 40).

One of the common traditional ways of expressing these beliefs is by worshiping God the Creator (Ngai Mumbi) and venerating ancestral spirits as well other anonymous spirits in various traditional shrines. Traditional form of worship is carried out in time of need especially during drought and famine, before planting and after harvesting among other occasions. Rituals also express the beliefs that Akamba people have for example, cleansing rituals done on an individual or family basis as prescribed by the diviner. In the traditional setting, rituals were viewed as an expression of the people's desire to maintain harmony with the spiritual world. In order to maintain this unity the traditional Akamba consulted diviners who were believed to possess the power to unveil the mysteries of life.

Although some of the Akamba today still express their traditional beliefs through traditional ways of worship, most of them prescribe to Christian worship. Christians worship God through prayers, offerings, and works of mercy, but above all, by celebrating the Eucharist. In Christian worship rituals are also a common expression of unity with God. Although people are invited to worship God as individuals or groups within the week, Sunday is generally the official day of Christian worship. However, some Christians such as the Seventh Day Adventist pray on Saturday. The Catholic Church, however, has some additional days of obligation such as Christmas, Easter, All Saints Day (1st November), All souls day (2nd November) and the Assumption of our Lady into Heaven (15th August).

Among the traditional Akamba there were different categories of specialists namely: diviners, priests, prophets, rainmakers and herbalists (Gehman, 2002:77). Although every specialist played a key role in the life of the community, the role of the diviner seemed to draw much more the attention of the people than that of other specialists. In his reflection on the African diviner, Zahan (1979:81) refers to the African universe as one that speaks to its people. He maintains that what the universe communicates to individuals and to the community is best accessed by religious specialists particularly the diviners.

Speaking of the Akamba situation, Baur (1990: 44) maintains that at the time missionaries entered Machakos in 1912, the Akamba were very strongly attached to their traditions, the fear of witchcraft was all pervading, and the Kamba witch-doctors were near and far recognized as the most powerful that even today they are still consulted. Baur's usage of the term witch-doctor to describe the Akamba diviner is not agreeable to this researcher. The term presupposes that the word diviner is synonymous to witch-doctor which is not the case. It is more acceptable to use the term diviner and not witch-doctor. Moreover, other than being derogative, the term witch-doctor is narrow and limiting compared to the people's understanding of the diviner's role. Witchcraft is only one among many other issues dealt with by diviners. Therefore this study prefers to use the term diviners due to the complex role they play among the people as will be seen in the chapters ahead.

What Baur observed many years back is not far from the researcher's observations which in turn motivated the study namely;

1) That some Akamba Christians continued to consult diviners for various reasons. A case narrated to the researcher by Patricia Mwanthi about Beata, a fellow Small Christian Community member was that she and her family consulted a diviner in 2006 during the illness of her daughter in law. In October 2007 Beata voluntarily mentioned to the researcher that she had severally consulted diviners in the past but that she had since then stopped the practice. During this conversation, she also narrated how she coincidently met a fellow Christian Angelina at the home of the same diviner. The researcher came to learn that Angelina herself had already

6

confessed to some members of her Small Christian Community of her involvement with diviners and how she coincidently met Beata in the home of the same diviner. She had been undergoing economic difficulties with none of her children holding a salaried job hence her decision to visit a diviner.

2) The researcher observed that in their preaching, some of the preachers tended to mention diviners from time to time. This mostly occurred whenever Christians were put on spot for their decline in faith. Furthermore, whenever consultation of diviners was mentioned there was laughter and murmurs from the faithfuls. These reactions led to many questions in the mind of the researcher. For one I kept wondering about the meaning of this laughter. The question as to whether those who reacted in this manner would be familiar with the issue of diviners kept rotating in my mind. The desire to know the truth other than speculate pushed me to this investigation.

3) The researcher listened to some preachers challenging the Christians about their wavering faith pinpointing reversion to traditional beliefs by consulting diviners. For example, in one of his Sunday homilies in the year 2005, Fr. Yusufu expressed his disappointment that some Christians instead of placing their full trust in Christ sought refuge in some traditional specialists in an effort to cleanse themselves from witchcraft. Later it became clear to the researcher that he was making reference to the traditional rituals of *ngata* that had become rampant at the time. The diviner carries out this kind of a ritual to disarm witches. One again the question in the mind of the researcher was, by whose powers would a diviner destroy witchcraft powers and why should Christians bow to such rituals?

4) Over a period of time, the researcher had observed that Christians who had been involved with diviners became inactive in the Church. Emmangu a neighbour to the researcher was once a very active Church leader. Immediately she began consulting diviners she resigned from Small Christian community leadership. The same observation was made of Beata and Angelina who as already noted once met at the home of a diviner. Still the question in the mind of the researcher was what is it about the diviner that attracts even Church leaders?

5) In evangelization, the researcher observed that a negative picture of the diviner was presented to the people. They were presented as pagans, promoters of evil and as people to be avoided. Due to their lack of faith in Christ, they were presented as op-posers of the gospel. This view was confirmed by one of the diviners interviewed during this research (M. Mutio, personal communication, March 10, 2008). March 10). Asked to comment on the Christian view that diviners were pagans she retorted, "Christians say that we work in collaboration with the devil, but I have never seen one and would like to see how the devil looks like" Behind this study was the desire to know about the nature of a diviner. Mutio's reaction made the researcher realize the sharp conflict between the old and the new value systems i.e. the traditional African value system and the Christian value system. In the African traditional society there is no emphasis on the Devil while Christianity sees Satan as the source of evil. This implies that the question of the Devil is in the Christian world view and not in African world view. In the issue of a negative Christian view of the diviner, the researcher wondered why some Christians still consulted diviners if they truly believed that they had a connection with the Devil, hence the reason for this study.

8

6) Very little inculturation has been done in the area of traditional beliefs and practices. For example, traditional melodies and rhythms have been given a key place in liturgy but nothing is mentioned of traditional specialists. The need to understand why African diviners were not reflected in the issue of inculturation moved the researcher to carry out this study.

From the above observations, the researcher concluded that to some extent the community was still diviner active and friendly. This necessitated that a study be carried out to investigate into the reasons for this reality especially among Christians.

Statement of the problem

In the contemporary African society and in particular among the Christians of the Catholic Diocese of Machakos, there has been a growing concern over the continued interaction between diviners and some members of the Church. It has been observed that despite the many years of modernization, interaction with modern education, catechesis and evangelization, some of the Christians still sought the help of diviners whenever life became tough, when sickness invaded or when the farm and animals became unproductive. The question is, why are the Akamba, still attracted to the diviner? What need does the diviner fulfill in the contemporary Akamba community and in Africa as a whole? These important questions raised in this study were shared by a vast number of the Akamba. Responses to these pertinent questions will be of great benefit not only to the Church but also to the Akamba community as well as other African communities.

The Church needs information on the relevance of diviners to the contemporary Akamba community as she advances in her efforts to anchor people's faith in Christ, and in promoting moral values among the people. Over the years, the Government of Kenya has shown interest in the manner in which witchcraft related problems in the country are handled. On 26th January, 1999, a Divisional officer in Makueni County issued a etter of warning to the people in regard to witchcraft practices. Such concern was an indicator that this study is needed. Diviners among the Akamba are believed to posses the power to destroy the powers of a witch and to provide some curative prescriptions for those who have been bewitched. Christians are not immune to this belief either.

Several studies to investigate the cultural practices of the Akamba in relation to their Christian faith have been carried out for example, Ngundo (2001). This study was aimed at investigating the impact of the traditional ways of healing on evangelization in Machakos Diocese. However, none of the studies done addressed the issue of diviners adequately in relation to the significant role they play among the people. This study was therefore set to investigate the relevance of diviners in contemporary Akamba community with reference to the Catholics of Machakos Diocese.

Significance of the study

Literature review revealed that academic focus on diviners had not yet been widely explored among the Akamba. In this study therefore, the researcher focuses attention on the relevance of diviners and the role they play among the Christians of the Catholic Diocese of Machakos. The study has incorporated views of different categories of people among the Akamba. The study is timely in that, the knowledge acquired is hoped to become a source of enrichment to those who need it particularly new researchers in African cultural values. Further still, the study presents in-depth knowledge about the the nature and role of diviners in the day today lives of the people. Not only is this knowledge crucial to individuals in their academic quest but also adds to the existing body of knowledge on diviners in the academic arena.

Information on diviners as cultural specialists in the contemporary Akamba community is timely because this study was motivated by the researcher's experience of a growing need to "discover" why some Christians still visited diviners. Establishing knowledge as to why this is happening was hoped to benefit all those involved in the work of faith formation. It was the researcher's hope that this would facilitate the development of better evangelization skills for deeper growth in faith among priests, catechists, Church leaders and indeed the entire Christian community in Machakos County.

To the entire Christian community in Machakos and Africa as a whole, this study is handy because it states that although the diviner is an important person in the culture, Christians have a more important person; Christ on whom their faith should be anchored. The informative sharing with respondents and written sources have revealed new knowledge on the state of Christian faith in Machakos Diocese. This study therefore proposes as a way forward a re-examination of the current methods of evangelization, conscientization seminars and workshops for the clergy, religious men and women and laity in the Diocese on traditional cultural values, beliefs and practices. The purpose for this is to equip agents of evangelization with clear knowledge about the old value system (African traditional culture) and how this differs from or relates to the new value system (Christianity).

Information on the relevance of diviners in the contemporary Akamba community is highly needed by the Government. Past experiences indicate that Government administrators have been concerned with matters of traditional practices among the people, which attest to their need of further knowledge and even clarification on certain issues which they often battle with. These include family conflicts which arise as a result of witchcraft allegations. For some of the Akamba, unless they have consulted a diviner, it is difficult for them to convict someone even though they may suspect him/her of being responsible for their problems. In such a case, the diviner plays the role of revealing the culprit which more often than not stirs up fury in the families concerned calling for government intervention hence the need for this study.

The significance of this study lies in what the researcher suggests that the activities of the diviner and their influence on the contemporary Akamba society should not be underrated. It has been the experience of the researcher that when diviners are mentioned, some Christians brush it off regarding them as old fashioned, while others still believe in them. It is more dangerous for Christians to ignore the activities of diviners than to face them head on. This study recommends that, interest to learn more about diviners and their activities should be cultivated today more than ever so as to understand more clearly that which in the diviner attracts people to them. Knowledge leads to informed and firm decisions especially about Christian faith.

Conceptual frame work

The conceptual framework of this study was based on the traditional African understanding of the diviner as a key figure in the life of the community. For example, Mbiti (1995: 177) points to the African diviner as an agent of unveiling mysteries in human. The contemporary Akamba have their share in this view. As a result, the study identifies several factors that are responsible for the value the Akamba attach to the diviner. Some of them are: The Akamba concept of diviners, Peoples' understanding of their traditional beliefs and practices, Methods of divination, Methods of evangelization and external pressure. These elements contribute in one way or another to the continued Christian involvement with diviners in the Catholic Diocese of Machakos. The dependent variable of this study is the relevance of diviners in the contemporary Akamba community. For the people to continue consulting the diviner there must be a motivating factor that constantly draws them there without which there would be no need for further visits. The figure below demonstrates the relationship between the dependent (the caused) and the independent (the cause) variables.

Figure 1: Relationship among variables

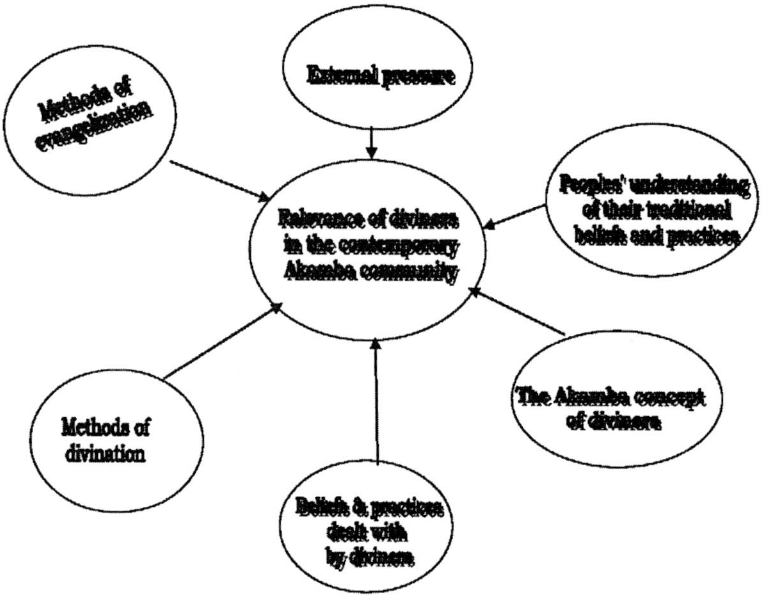

Scope and delimitations of the study

The relevance of diviners in contemporary Akamba community is core to this study. The choice of the topic was anchored on its perceived ability to provide answers to the current concern among a number of Catholics in Machakos Diocese that consult diviners. For the purpose of quality, clarity and coherence, this study concentrates on Machakos Catholic diocese.

This study is limited to two main religions namely; African traditional religion and Christianity. The researcher has interacted more with traditional worshipers and Christians than with members of other faiths such as Islam. Among the Christians of Machakos, the preferred group was Catholic to which the researcher belongs. This deliberate limitation was based on the fact that, when one deals with familiar concepts there is a higher possibility of describing items with more clarity and surety, avoiding assumptions or generalizations while at the time retaining sensitivity.

According to political and colonial boundaries, "Ukamba" is divided into West and East. The West is occupied by the Akamba of Kitui while the East is occupied by the Akamba of Machakos. Between the two groups of Akamba, there exists a difference in cultural beliefs and practices as well. This difference is experienced in the language use where by some words may mean something different for instance; the word used for stealing in Kitui is *kung'ea* while in Machakos it is *kuya*. Another difference occurs in beliefs and their practices. For example, among the Akamba of Kitui, grandchildren celebrate the death of their grandparents, scramble for inheritance and have an upper hand in the burial preparations. This practice which the researcher witnessed in Kimangao in Kitui is unheard of in Machakos. The Akamba of Machakos of whom the researcher is part, have a common interpretation of most cultural elements. They use the same dialect hence the choice to carry out the study among them for the purpose of coherence. This limitation is also aimed at enabling the researcher to concentrate on a workable area size for quality purpose.

Operational definition of terms

Diviner - A traditional specialist consulted on a variety of culturally related matters such as illness, continuous misfortunes and broken taboos among others.

Sorcerer- man or woman who uses material objects to cause harm to another or to his/her property

Witch- A person who uses evil powers, inherent or acquired to cause harm to others and their possessions

Witchcraft- an evil power in a person believed to cause harm to people and their possessions

Culture - Is the sum total of all realities of a given society which include among others customs, language, beliefs and practices, norms and religion

Belief - A belief is a mental attitude of acceptance of something as right or wrong, true or false.

Medicine man/woman- One who in the African traditional society specializes in diagnosis and treatment of various ailments by use of herbal medicine

Shrine - In this study the term shrine is used to refer to a traditional place of worship such as under the *Muumo* tree among the Akamba.

Taboo - Something that is forbidden by the culture

Oath - A solemn vow

Ritual - An outward expression of a popular action which is performed individually or communally as need arises for example, a healing ritual

Evangelization- Comes from the Greek word 'evangelion' which means good news. Evangelization is therefore the act of bringing good news into all strata of humanity. In the context of this study evangelization is understood as the proclamation of the values of Jesus Christ to the people in order that they may make a personal decision to follow him.

CHAPTER TWO: THE AKAMBA PEOPLE OF KENYA: AN OVERVIEW

Introduction

This chapter underlines key aspects in the life of the Akamba people without which the context of this study would not be concretely placed. The significance of this chapter lies in the fact that, understanding the history of a people enables others to understand why they hold certain beliefs and behave in a certain manner. Knowledge of the history of a people highly contributes to the appreciation of their spiritual, moral and social thought. This chapter is pertinent to the study because it prepares the ground for a better understanding of contemporary Akamba. By familiarizing with the background of the Akamba, one may find it easier to understand why some of their belief systems have remained significant to the people even after many years of evangelization. The chapter comprises two main sections. Section one exposes the historico-social background information of the Akamba. Under this, the following areas have been discussed: Geographical setting of the Akamba, historical setting, the Akamba community set up, political organization and economic activities. Section two discusses the Akamba cosmology and consists of the following areas: traditional religion and Christianity; mysticism; the Akamba traditional specialists and the human person. In view of the current faith situation among the Akamba, it stands out clearly that traditional religion is still alive while majority of the people profess Christianity as already pointed out. This was also confirmed during the field study. During the field study the researcher discovered that in every family of a diviner, traditional worshiper or a traditional elder visited, there were Christians as well. It would therefore have limited this study too much if the two religions were not taken into consideration.

Historico-social background information of the Akamba

Geographical Setting

As already noted, generally the Akamba are found in the Eastern part of Kenya, Eastern Province. These people are Bantu speaking people and Kikamba is their main language. According to Lindblom (1969: 22), "Ukamba" is divided into two main parts, the upper (ulu) which lies to the west of Athi River and the East Ukambani located at the East. The upper part is generally referred to as the Ukamba of Kitui while the East is the Ukamba of Machakos. The upper part lies between an average height of about 1500 meters above sea level while the East Ukamba is less than 1000 meters above sea level whereas. The Akamba are the fourth largest ethnic group in Kenya. Fedders (1994: 20) postulated that they total roughly to 1.2 million. Ukamba consists of numerous mountain chains from north to south which intersect it. Within the highest peaks is Nzaui hill at Kilungu. According to the legend, the first people lived there (Lindblom, 1969: 22).

There are numerous streams and rivers but most of them are seasonal except Tana and Athi rivers. During the dry seasons, people have to dig some large holes in the dried up river beds in search of water. Drought is a common experience among these people. Much of Ukambani is dry but fertile especially during rain seasons. There are two main rainy seasons: a lesser one is in November-December while a greater, season which begins from March to May (Lindblom 1969: 23). Although Lindblom claims that this season lasts up to June, it is worthy noting that, there have been great climatic changes since his time. The reverse has actually happened. Currently, the Akamba have a better harvest in the first season which commences in November extending to January, than in the second (March - May). Despite the rainfall fluctuations, the Akamba can rightly be called agriculturalists as will be discussed later in this chapter.

Histirical setting

Akamba theories of origin

Despite their geographical divisions, the Akamba share a common history as discussed in a number of theories.

Theory one: The Akamba myth of origin states that, *Mulungu* (God) created man and woman and tossed them from heaven to the earth. They landed on a stone on the hills of Nzaui, Kilungu. The theory states that they formed the first clan known as '*Mbai ya mulata ivia*' (the clan that landed on a stone). *Mulungu* created livestock and tossed these to the earth too. He caused very heavy rains till the earth was filled with ant-hills from which came another man and woman. The new couple from the ant-hills had daughters while the one tossed from heaven had sons. Their children intermarried. God loved them and blessed them with plenty of food, cattle, sheep and goats. They sacrificed to God regularly. At one time they forgot to sacrifice to God and this made Him very angry to the extent of denying them rain. As a result, severe famine struck, leading people to migrate to other places in search of better livelihood. The immigrants became Ameru, Agikuyu, Aembu, and Maasai. The ones who survived the tragedy are the Akamba (Lindblom 1969: 12).

Theory two: A second theory locates the ancient home of the Akamba down towards the coast in the neighborhood of the Agiriama (Lindblom 1969: 14). According to this theory, from Giriama at the coastal area of Kenya they moved to a place known as Mbooni at the south of Machakos town. From there they are said to have dispersed with time to different directions (Ndeti, 1972: 1). Evidence to this is the fact that all Ukambani clans trace their origin from Mbooni. Villages of Mbooni are named according to the clans which occupy them. These villages include Utangwa the village occupied by *Atangwa*, Kitondo occupied by *Akitondo*, Iuani occupied by *Auani*, Kaumoni occupied by *Aumoni*, Nziu occupied by *Anziu*, Mutwii occupied by *Atwii* and Kisau occupied by *Anzauni*. Migrations from these sites are said to have been triggered by the search for water, food and better pastures (Musembi, 1999: 13). However, due the great famine experienced in 1836, the Akamba are said to have had further migrations to various locations.The fact that the Akamba lived elsewhere is be evidenced by the presence of Kamba villages around Mt. Kilimanjaro, between Taveta and Lake Jipe, to the south of Pare Mountains and Usambara Mountains.

Theory three: A more popular theory traces the origin of the Akamba people from Tanganyika (Tanzania) around Mt. Kilimanjaro, where they are believed to have been part of the Nyamwezi ethnic group. This theory suggests that, migration from this area was probably triggered by pressure from the Maasai who had already settled in this area. In-fact up to this day, the Akamba and Maasai around Sultan Hamud fight from time to time over land issues.

From the above theories we realize that although the Akamba may be termed as one ethnic community, a few differences can be noted among them. Basically, the Akamba of Machakos differ form the Akamba of Kitui in terms of linguistic code. The Akamba of Kitui found to the west of Athi River, are commonly referred to as the "*Ulu*" Akamba while those in the East are the

Akamba of Machakos. The dialect spoken by the Akamba of Kitui is referred to as "*Kithaisu*" and is quite different from the one spoken by the Akamba of Machakos. Nevertheless, it is notable that today there is more interaction between the two groups than before which has led to considerable appreciation and understanding of each other's dialect. This interaction has contributed to the integration of the two dialects especially through reading some common literature such as the Bible. In class one and two, pupils in primary schools across the two districts read the same kikamba books. Further still, most of the Church literature in Kikamba has been written by the Akamba of Kitui for example; '*Mukilisito wa'wo*' (comprises both instructional material and prayers for daily use) and other spiritual literature.

The Akamba community set up

The Akamba community set up includes both the social structure and the kinship lineage. According to Mutuku (1992: 8) the Akamba social structure begins with the family (Musyi) as the basic social unit, be it monogamous or polygamous. Next to *Musyi* is the clan (mbai). A clan consists of both close and distant relatives of the father's lineage. Clan names according to Lindblom (1969: 114) bear the name of the founding ancestor. This could be his real name, nick name or the name of his area. Lindblom (1969: 136) further notes that each clan has a totem for example, *Amumoni*- the wild fig (mumo), *Akitutu*- the Hawk (Mbolosya), *Amuuti*-the secretary bird (Ndei). The clan is followed by a territorial unit known as hamlet (utui) which is a group of neighbours living close to each other. Several hamlets form a *kivalo*. The kinship lineage can be summarized as follows: Family (Musyi) ► Clan (Mbai) ► Hamlet (Kivalo)

Another social structure among the Akamba is determined by rank and age and is hierarchical by nature. It begins from the youngest member of the community to the oldest as follows: *kana* (a child) ▶ *Mwanake* a young unmarried man and *Mwiitu* a young unmarried girl ▶ *Nthele* a young married man ▶ *Mutumia* an elderly married man, *Kiveti* a married woman (young or old but one who has had children). Among men, two types of elders are identified in the highest rank namely, the council of elders (Atumia ma nzama) and the top most elders (atumia ma mutwe). Since one has to surrender ten goats and two bulls to the council of elders for initiation into the second rank, not many make it to this level. Elders in the second category play the role of shrine elders (Atumia ma Ithembo). These are elderly men who concern themselves with worship in the shrines. They organize, guard and maintain them. For one to be allowed to the altar, he ought to have undergone the final rituals of elder-hood (kukula). According to one of the interviewees, although he was a ritual elder before his conversion to Catholic faith, he had not undergone the final rituals and therefore could not access the altar. His role was to hand to the chief elder the foods and meat prepared for the sacrifice (M. Mwangu, personal communication, March 14, 2008).

An elder is identified by the symbols of a stool (Muumbu) and a staff (Ndata ya maka). For one to become an elder in the traditional sense he has to make some payment to the other elders who then hold an inaugural ceremony. Although previous writers including Lindblom saw elder-hood as an enterprise of the living, the researcher wishes to add that, becoming an ancestor among the Akamba is the highest rank of existence. So to speak, the ritual elders perform their duties with high esteem and reverence to ancestral spirits. Provision of cooked food stuffs and libations are a physical indication of an intimate encounter with the spirits during and after the ritual. Ancestors are, therefore, senior to elders hence the reason why elders work very closely with them.

Political organization

Traditionally, a patriarchal form of government existed long before the onset of colonial rule in Kenya. Although the Akamba had no chiefs, each village had its own council of elders (Nzama ya ndua) for the maintenance of law and order (Lindblom, 1969: 150). Village elders had nothing to do with the official community ranking mentioned above. This group which comprised elderly respectful men in the village was concerned with matters of general welfare of the community. The government today uses the same elders to reach out to community members. For matters that are legal in nature, a special group comprising the larger clan members (mbai nene) known as *king'ole* (Kamba high court) came together to decide on particular cases such as: witchcraft, sorcery or rape. In raiding, the young unmarried men (anake) and the young married men (nthele) formed the raiding unit with *Muthiani* as their leader (Mutuku, 1992: 8). However, today these traditionally formed groups are no longer as active as before. This is due to reinforcement of administrative laws of the country.

Economic activities

The Akamba are identified with farming despite erratic rainfalls. Farming includes planting crops such as maize, beans, sorghum, millet, cassava, sweet potatoes and pumpkins among others. In some areas coffee and pyre thrum are grown as cash crops. They also keep cattle, goats, sheep and chicken. In the olden days, the bigger the herd the more prestigious the family felt. Families today keep fewer animals owing to reduced ancestral lands coupled with poor rains. For income generation, some people make ropes out of sisal, women weave baskets while men engage in sand harvesting and wood carving among other supplementary activities. Since most of the Akamba have no cash crops, whatever little food they harvest is divided between consumption and sale. However, with the introduction of better scientific ways of farming, some people are now practicing horticulture but only on small scale basis. This involves planting fruits such as papaws, oranges, mangoes and lemons to mention a few. Those living near river banks have also resolved to planting vegetables such as cabbages, tomatoes, onions and *sukuma wiki*. Although many parts of Ukambani are relatively dry, some people are turning to tree planting. Eventually, these become a source of income in terms of providing building material and charcoal burning. Through this effort, some parents have been able to educate their children.

Having provided some background information on the Akamba people, the proceeding discussions in this chapter explores some key elements that make up the Akamba world view. These include the peoples understanding of the human person in relation to the universe around him, various traditional specialists and the role they play in a bid to enhance harmony in the universe, the belief and practice of traditional religion in the traditional setting, its continuity today and the renaissance of Christianity. The birth of Christianity among the Akamba not only effected change among its adherents about the understanding of the spiritual world around them but also created a conflict of belief.

Akamba cosmology

The Human Being in the Universe

The Akamba refer to the human person as *mundu*. They believe that *mundu* was created by God (Ngai Mumbi). According to Ndeti (1972:28), God created man and woman and brought them from the sky to this earth. The existence of the Akamba in the universe is therefore in harmony with God's plan and purpose.

Gehman observes that the Akamba concept of the human person trascends the two realities of a person; body and soul. *Mundu* among the Akamba is a community (Gehman, 1989:56). This community extends beyond the living members of the clan or ethnic community to the ancestral world as well as that of the unborn. In agreement with Gehman, Ndeti (1972: 114) sees *mundu* as experiencing the three life cycles; life, spirit and immortality. The researcher is in harmony with these views because the Akamba do not only see their origin nor destiny in what is here and now but readily in what was there and is to come. At death, though the body diminishes the spirit forges ahead to the spirit world while at the same time maintaining links with kinship members. It is at this point that *mundu* is counted a living dead. This is because despite their spiritual status they still continue to influence the life of their living family members.

In the Akamba community, the human person is never viewed as an individual but as a corporate member of the community (Gehman, 1989: 51). The human person depends on the community for survival, care and growth. Without intimacy with the community, the individual loses direction and sense of

25

purpose. Both the individual and the community strive towards the experience of unity. It is on this basis that Mbiti assertively postulates, "I am, because we are; and since we are, therefore I am" (Mbiti, 1995: 104).

Because life in the community is a collective experience, on its part, the community places some checks and balances in form of rules that govern human relationships. According to Durkheim (1963:114), human relations are seen in terms of clashing intentions which society at best can regulate but never suppress. In this case, moral rules are invested with a special authority by virtue of which they are obeyed simply because they command. Rebellion against the traditional morality is perceived by some as a revolt of the individual against collective morality. According Durkheim, obligation is one of the primary characteristics of moral rule. In this case, taboos among the Akamba were seen as an effective means by which collective behaviour was regulated for the purpose of maintaining cosmological balance. For example, it is taboo for a daughter in-law to enter the bedroom of her parents' in-law or greet her father-in-law by a hand shake. It was also taboo for a pregnant woman to touch a corpse (Lindblom, 1969: 101-105). Failure to observe the collective morality made manifest through taboos, was believed to cause problems to those concerned. At times the cause of a problem may not be clear to the victim or victims to a point at which some people seek the intervention of a diviner for clarity.

Among the Akamba, the collective voice is superior to that of the individual. Berger (1967: 81) in his sociological theory points out that society is a product of collective activity. In this case, an individual may find him/herself drawn towards that which the community upholds despite his/her desire to follow his/her own choice. This is because his/her active participation is demanded by the community for continued construction of the community. This observation by Berger helps us understand why cases of Christians being forced into traditional rituals have always succeeded. According to Berger, due to the inevitable links of the individual with others in society, the individual has to reckon with society as a hard reality.

In the Akamba community, the human person is at the center of the universe. God is outside it and beyond it (Mbiti, 1992: 43). For the Akamba, the human person is the wisest creature among all others. He/she is fully aware of his/her responsibility to contribute to universal harmony. According to Durkheim (1963: 114), the human person must work hard towards this goal because society transcends the individual. Society in this case is the end of all moral activity. Being at the center of the universe, the human person experiences the universe in a personal way. In this way, he/she enjoys from the universe both material and spiritual benefits. He/she sees the universe in his/her own perspective and endeavours to live in harmony with it.

In order to maintain harmony in the universe, good care is taken in all relationships, both with the spiritual world and with one another. In this case, people try not to offend the deities as this would result into imbalance in the universe, causing them to suffer. This harmony is both vertical and horizontal. In their day to day living, people must maintain a harmonious relationship among them by observing the norms governing life in the community.

In the universe, the human person is part of nature and at the same time the product of cultural existence. Rousseau (in Bidney, 1996: 13) says "Man is born free but is every where in chains" This statement points to a real human situation in that although one wishes to lead a unique life in the society, more often than not, his/her ambitions are thwarted by the community's demands to: gather together, work together, laugh and mourn together. Among the Akamba, community activities such as those related to marriage preparations and funerals stand strong to date.

Another outstanding element in the Akamba understanding of the human person is the responsibility to participate in the continuity of community life. Among the traditional Akamba community, marriage was the one means by which this participation could be brought to completion.

Among the Akamba, the human person is very important so much so that every activity is geared towards his/her welfare. In this context, the diviner is seen by many of the Akamba as a necessary person in the effort to promote human life. This view which is shared by many traditional Akamba is one that has promoted the diviners' activities among the people.

The Akamba traditional specialists

Among the Akamba there are different specialists. These people are believed to possess one kind or more of mystical powers. On the whole, these specialists function to enhance harmony among individuals and in the community as a whole. It is their duty in their diversity to ensure harmony in the universe.

Medicine men/women- They concern themselves with the health of individuals and of the community. Medicine practitioners vary according to their preferred methods. Majority of them make use of herbs both for physical and emotional healing. Ndeti says "The medicine man is dedicated to the care of the sick through the use of local herbs" (1972: 116). Under both circumstances rituals may be performed either in the preparation of the medicine or in the healing process. Some herbalists among the Akamba at times play the role of a diviner.

Prophets- These are people who foretell about the future such as an impending disaster. Gehman (1989: 88) postulates that *Kathambi* (a certain spirit) appears to prophets in their sleep and passes some message to them. Some pronounced Kamba prophets were Syokimau, Syokaiku, Syondonga and Syenze (Gehman 1989: 89).

Diviners- Some scholars such as Lindblom (1969: 258) and Gehman (1989: 86) writing about the Akamba diviner claim that the name diviner is synonymous to medicine man/woman. However, the researcher does not concur with them because, not all diviners are medicine men/women and not all medicine men/women qualify as diviners. Though closely linked we have to treat them as two distinct specialists. The name *Mundu mue* means a wise or shrewd person. In Kikamba, the word wisdom is *ui*. A diviner is regarded as a wise person shown in the manner he/she handles clients, the tactiful way in which he/she integrates human and esoteric virtues while dealing with complicated cases as well as following complicated procedures to arrive at desired solutions to human problems. Gehman (1989: 86) comments that, basic to the Akamba world view is the cosmological balance between good and evil. The witch who employs the powers of witchcraft represents evil within the created universe. Counter balancing this is the diviner who employs the greater powers of divination (uwe) to confront evil in society.

Medicine men and women among the Akamba are revered as healers; a role that is chiefly achieved through herbs, hence the name herbalists (Akimi ma miti). More often than not, these people have nothing to do with divination powers or skills. My own grandfather (my mother's father) was a well known traditional medicine man who purely dealt with herbs. Up to the time of his death in 1988, he was still a strong practitioner and a staunch Catholic as well. Some diviners can also act as specialists in traditional medicine. My grandmother (my father's mother) was one of these rare diviners up to the time of her death in 1987. Traditionally, diviners (Awe) were the only people at whose houses the *kilumi* dances would be carried out and not in the houses of medicine men/women. This was a strong point of distinction between the two specialists. The reason for this is that diviners are associated with clairvoyance and so people go to them in search of some communication from the spirit world. One of the renowned *kilumi* dancers in Ikalaasa revealed that one major reason as to why they danced from the home of diviners was to in order to enquire about the on-going issues in the community, receive new revelations from the spirit world and to seek direction on the waqy forward. (K. Mulwa, personal communication, March 16, 2008). According to Kitulya Mulwa, if instructions were keenly followed all would be well in the community and vice versa. This practice existed long before Christianity spread in Ukambani and still continues in some parts to date.

Nature of the Akamba Diviner

In Mbiti's view (1992: 177), a diviner is an agent of unveiling mysteries of life. In order to serve this purpose for the good of the community, diviners depend primarily on divination. Divination is done through the use of mediums, oracles, being possessed, divination objects, common sense, intuitive knowledge and insight, hypnotism, and other secret knowledge. He further notes that, divination is done by means of pebbles, numbers, water, animal entrails, reading the palm and by throwing dice among many other methods. Mbiti (1992: 157) asserts that diviners are people with a language of their own.

The Akamba hold a strong belief in the existence of a spiritual world around them whereby God and all other spiritual beings live. Along with this belief is the great awareness of the presence of forces of evil that often destabilize both individual and communal harmony. The Akamba have a very strong sense of their human nature that makes them vulnerable as creatures. In their effort to achieve harmony with the spiritual world, many things go wrong that bring about disharmony and undesired imbalance. For example, disobedience to community norms such as, breaking a taboo is an offense to the ancestors. Once there is imbalance in peoples' lives, a lot of suffering that is physical, psychological, social, economic and moral is believed to surface. Because of the ambiguity of these states, a diviner is more often than not found necessary to bring things to light and to provide answers for these complex situations.

Among the Akamba, diviners act as:
1) Integral healers- Once the problem has been diagnosed, what follows is the practical application of the prescribed cure. Under normal circumstances, the cure depends on the cause of the problem such as:
    a) Witchcraft- The diviner who is an expert, will, through the application of various methods determine who for example, the witch is. According

to Mbula, witchcraft can cause physical harm to human beings, animals or crops and can burn buildings down. (Mbula, 1982: 104) In this case, healing may be effected through cleansing and health rituals, libations, wearing a particular cloth to ward off these powers or being in possession of any other object issued by the diviner.

b) Insulting or dishonoring a deity in which case some form of placation may be carried out.

c) Breaking an oath, taboo or curse may also cause trouble to an individual and his family members. According to Ndeti (1972: 116) cleansing rituals may be carried out by the diviner to break the negative force. At other times healing may be effected by atonement and restoration into the good graces of the family and community through a ritual.

2) Defenders of the community against evil powers. In this case, people visit them to obtain preventive charms against witches and other evil forces. It was a common practice in the Kamba traditional community for a diviner to be invited to seal the homestead with his/her medicine through a ritual designed for that purpose (mbingo). This was done by burying a pot at the main entrance to the homestead containing some objects prepared by the diviner. Other items treated by the diviner were also planted at various corners around the homestead. This ritual was done to prevent evil people such as witches and sorcerers from affecting the family members with their evil powers.

3) Mediums- In this case he/she acts as mediator between the living and the living dead. In the traditional Kamba community whenever people wish to communicate with the ancestors they pass through these wise men and women in the community.

4) Consultants -In the traditional setting a diviner is consulted in the

32

perplexing occasions of life. In this case, he/she plays the role of a counselor as well as an advisor. As a counselor, he/she listens to people's stories and gives them the necessary guidance. As advisors, diviners lead their clients to face the reality presented in their problems and guide them to adopt solutions best suited to these problems.

From the various scholars writing about the Akamba the indication is that, diviners play a vital role in the life of the community. They fulfill an intermediary function between the physical and the psychical and between the physical and the spiritual for the sake of the community. Diviners welcome all kinds of people who wish to consult them since they are there for the community. However, as noted earlier, the continued presence of these traditional specialists among the people has been an area of concern for the Church. With some Christians being attracted to the diviner it poses the challenge of dualism. During the field study, all the diviners interviewed confirmed that a good number of their clients were Christians. This issue will be discussed further in chapter five and six.

Mysticism in the Akamba community

Belief in mystical powers is a dominant feature of the Akamba world view. Gehman (1989: 80) observed that though the Akamba cannot explain its nature or source, they can reiterate experience after experience of the reality of this power. He further remarks "this inexplicable power is resident in plant and animal life, manifested through spoken words and mediated through specialists" This explains why the Akamba make use of certain plants such as *mutaa* for cleansing and healing purposes. Among the Akamba, mystical power is made manifest in two main ways; witchcraft and divination.

Belief in witchcraft is driven by the belief that some people possess an intrinsic power, inherited, inborn or acquired that can be released at will to cause harm to an intended victim. Among the Akamba witches tend to utilize items that had once been in contact with the person such as hair, finger nails and private parts such as breasts (Gehman, 1989: 82). These are mixed with other ingredients to form potent witchcraft. Hobley (1910: 93) points to the practice of taking the footprints of a person, cow dung or chicken waste (kuuta kiunya) to treat secretly for evil purposes. In the practice of witchcraft, charms are used. By charms we mean the use of materials that have gone through the secret ritual of a witch to cause negative effects on another person or his property.

The second type of mystical power is divination (uwe). This type of mystical power is viewed as beneficial because it is utilized to reveal secret knowledge. Among the Akamba, the diviner comes in to respond to the question, "why?" This is due to the elaborate traditional belief that nothing happens for no reason. In divination, one articulates the epistemology of a people (Peek, 1991: 2). In more specific terms, divination can be described as that process by which a problem is diagnosed and solutions sought. In this process, diviners endeavor to answer the question 'why' and 'what' which happen to be the most crucial questions in times of crisis among Africans. For example, why me? Why my child? why this time?, why this animal? (Gehman, 1989: 86) Once the cause of the problem has been established, the next question that the diviner must answer is "what can I do?" Without a clear solution to the disturbing issue, the client's mission is not yet done and may be the cause for a visit to a different diviner at the cost of the former diviner's credibility. In divination therefore, one makes effort to do all that is possible to the benefit of his/her client. The diviner conveys not his/her own opinions to his/her clients but communicates messages from the spirit world.

Late 1980's, on one Sunday afternoon, the researcher in the company of other youths became curious about some women traditional dancers in the compound of one of the community diviners. In the midst of loud drums and song, these women spoke strange languages, yawned, cried out loudly and some of them jumped up and down while others stepped on burning fire without being burned. The diviner shook hands with each of them three times while at the same time inquiring from the possessing spirit what it wanted from the person. To each spirit the promise to fulfill its demands was made by the diviner. This went on for quite a while after which there was calmness followed by a less vigorous dance. According to the *kilumi* dancers, spirits poses people as a way of interacting with them as well as making their needs known to them. At this juncture it is important to note that *kilumi* dances take place in the house of a diviner unless some one needs to have it in their house as a healing ritual which is rare. *Kilumi* dancers believe that fulfillment of the spirits' needs bestows harmony in the community. This belief is the stronghold of traditional religion as will be noted in the following discussions.

Traditional religion of the Akamba

The Akamba in the traditional setting did not exhibit a dichotomy between the profane and the sacred, between religion and culture. Their belief is ultimately expressed in the Akamba creed already referred to in chapter one, in which confession of knowledge of God is made (Mbula, 1982: 40). Here God is recognized as Creator and sustainer of all that exists.

Belief in the Supreme Being

The Akamba world view would not suffice without the mention of the Supreme Being. Ndeti (1972: 175) writing on the Akamba beliefs and practices declares, "The notion of a personal God is extremely naïve and does not make sense in the Akamba belief". Another author Muthiani (1973: 98) writes:

> To some degree the Akamba are monotheists in that they have the concept of the one Supreme Being they call *Mulungu*. On the other hand, their religious practices revealed a belief in three gods- the creator, the splinter and *Mulungu*. They rationalized that the job of the Creator was to create man and everything else; the splinter would come along and split the limbs, fingers, tree branches, leaves of plants and everything that gives form to all that exists. But the splinter and the Creator are stewards of *Mulungu*.

Although Muthiani seems to point to a Trinitarian concept of God among the Akamba, the researcher does not see this thought having any practical backing in the traditional setting. In their view of God, the Akamba did hold belief in a Supreme Being with whom there was very little interaction. This Supreme Being is responsible for the emergence of all that exists. In this case, the Akamba name this Supreme Being according to their understanding of His nature and the various roles He accomplishes in the community. As one listens to various opinions, it is worthy noting that there are some commonly accepted concepts of God among the Akamba. The traditional names given to God are:

a. **Mulungu**- This name is derived from the Bantu languages. The name *Mulungu* is closely linked to *Mungu* in Kiswahili which denote a High God, worthy of honour and adoration.

b. **Mumbi**- *Mumbi* means 'Creator' derived from the verb *kumba* 'to create'. The name *Mumbi* is usually preceded by the name *Ngai* hence the terms *Ngai Mumbi* 'God the Creator', the one who brings life into existence, shapes and fashions what he has made.

c. To these two terms is added a third one **Mwatuang*i*** meaning 'the cleaver'. This does not denote three gods as Muthiani claims. Instead, the two terms *Mumbi* and *Mwatuangi* connote and emphasize on the unique activity of *Ngai* or *Mulungu* of bringing into existence the human person and all that exists in the universe. The name *Ngai* is also used for lesser spirits such as gods of the traveler (ngai sya muviti) and the family gods (ngai sya musyi). The use of the word *ngai* to refer to the lesser spirits is distinguished by its plural application i.e. *ngai sya* 'the gods of'. When the same word is used to refer to the Supreme Being it automatically takes on the noun *Mumbi* and so it becomes *Ngai Mumbi*. This term which refers to God the Creator always appears in the singular form and is an attribute of God. The different names therefore do not propose the presence of different gods. Mumbi and Mwatuangi are both attributes of God which denote His creative role.

Character of the Akamba God

The Akamba believe that God is transcendent and mysterious. This is because He stays alone and is unknowable. His dwelling place is '*ituni*' a place with no locality like cloud or sky. Ndeti states, "Thus *Mulungu* is an extremely impersonal force which is rarely mentioned or called upon for personal gains or triumphs (1972: 176). Because God is so great and mysterious, He is feared

37

above all else.

God is invisible because no one has ever seen Him, no one can curve Him. The Akamba as good as they are in curving, no one has ever tried to come up with an image of God. Despite his invisibility, He is both near and far. Mbiti (1995: 18) in an attempt to explain this paradox asserts that *Mulungu* is near in the sense that He is always accessible to the Akamba when they call on Him in prayer. But He is also far in the sense that He is not actively involved in the affairs of the people.

God is believed to know all things. The Akamba believe that no one can deceive or hide anything from *Mulungu* because he is full of wisdom and knowledge.

God is powerful. Since He is powerful He is capable of doing all things. The Akamba experience the power of God through the presence of mountains, rivers and trees such as the *muumo* tree. The Akamba believe that to be able to create such things, he must be a mighty God. Through his power, he causes mighty things to happen such as rain for continuity of biological life.

God is omnipresent, He is everywhere. Where ever a person is, he/she can call on God if need arises. The Akamba thus conceive of God's presence in terms of blessings and welfare. In the traditional Akamba community, when one had an accumulation of wealth in form of cattle, sheep, goats, wives and children, he was counted among the blessed ones or it was that God manifested through the things he possessed.

God is morally good, kind and loving. The goodness of God is practically experienced through the good acts he does towards his people for example, giving them rain and good harvest. Mbiti (1995: 37) says that the Akamba among other African communities view God as one who does to them only what is good.

Worship of God

Worship is the way through which African peoples respond to the spiritual world around them. Mbiti observes that this response takes on the form of worship which is expressed through a variety of acts and sayings. However, these vary from community to community (Mbiti, 1995: 58). Worship is uttered rather than meditational. It is also worthy noting that worship among the Akamba is more of a collective activity than personal and more public than private. However, personal effort to live in accordance with the community's demands enables one to remain in communion with the ancestors thus, leading to a life of blessings. Among the Akamba, children do not go to the shrine for worship. Worship is taken with great seriousness among adults. Only elderly men and women attend the shrine worship. "Those who participate in shrine worship must be people of integrity, people who understand the purpose of worship and that are disposed for it" (K.Kitulya, personal communication, March 17, 2008). According to Kitulya, if care is not taken God can be offended resulting into punishment of the entire community. In the opinion of traditional worshipers, prosperity of the community depends on the reverence accorded to God and the spirits. For this reason, children would be kept off to avoid their play, crying or any other form of distraction during worship. Worship in the shrines is, therefore, the obligation of married members of the community. This is because they are not only fully anchored in the community's affairs but also understand what worship is.

Writers on Akamba literature seem to be in agreement that the worship of God was based on need. Events of drought, famine, floods and epidemics among the people necessitated the plea for God's intervention. Mbiti (1995: 14) asserts that apart from the case of Christians, communication between human beings and God is very rare and if it happens it is of dire need. He further acknowledges that the Akamba, God's children, are used to living almost unconsciously without Him. Lindblom (1969: 144-145) as well observes "*Mulungu* is not worshiped at all or at least extremely seldom by offering sacrifices or in any other way". However, he cites examples of such moments that he witnessed the direct worship of *Mumbi* namely: at a child's birth, in request for rain and during a second circumcision rite whereby the leader of the ceremonies poured a little oil as an offering to *Mulungu*, at the same time sending up prayers that the novices might turn out well. Lindblom's statement that Mulungu is not worshiped at all is seen by the researcher as an overtone. Nevertheless, Gehman (1989: 202) affirms Mbiti's and Lindblom's view that the Akamba rarely worshiped God when he says that, the Akamba traditionally only worshipped God twice annually when all went well, namely, before the rains and after the harvest. He quotes the Akamba as saying "People do not go to the traditional shrine without a reason. God is never prayed for nothing. At another incident he quotes a practicing medicine man as declaring that he did not pray to *Ngai Mumbi* at all, but to the living dead.

Interviews conducted among several Akamba traditional worshipers established that shrine worship is still active in some places of Ikalaasa and Masinga. Kitulya who described himself as holding the office similar to that of a bishop seconded by Mwangu a former shrine elder informed the researcher that worship has to take place in September before the rains and after the first harvest between January and February. These elders shared that in time of drought, special prayers are held. In this case sheep is used for the sacrifice. According to one of the shrine elders, (I. Mutune, personal communication, March 20, 2008) a male sheep is slaughtered and some of its meat boiled while the rest is hang on the trees in the shrine for the spirits to have a share. The shrine is then covered with the contents of the large intestine (kuumba ithembo). This is in order to protect the community from illness and other calamities. Participants also take with them some of these contents to their homes and mix them with either drinking water or food for the same purpose. These elders confirmed that God was always pleased with the Akamba meaning that there was no need to disturb him with prayers unless this was really necessary.

The presence of traditional shrines known as *Mathembo* was an indication of the peoples' faith in God and spirits. These shrines still exist in many places to date. Sacrifices of animals and food offerings were the common expressions of the people's prayer to the spiritual beings. All the traditional worshipers interviewed were in agreement that at the shrine a goat and beer form part of the September worship while in the second worship cooked foods are added to the two. Lindblom (1969: 249) informs us that ancestral worship was the most outstanding form of worship among the Akamba. To this day, traditional worshipers are heard referring to the gods of the rivers, forests, travelers and of space.

Veneration of ancestors

Ancestral spirits or the living dead (aa umau maitu) are the souls of the departed of up to five generations. Mbiti describes them as those within the *sasa* period. They are in the state of personal immortality, and their process of dying is not yet complete, hence the term 'living dead' (1995: 83) He further comments:

> These are the spirits with which African people's are most concerned: it is through them that the spirit world becomes personal to men…they know and have interest in what is going on in the family…They are the guardians of family affairs, traditions, ethics and activities.

Gehman (1989: 151) identifies three types of ancestral spirits in the Kamba community:

1. The ancestral spirits of the homestead referred to as the "homestead gods" (ngai sya musyi)

2. The shepherd (Muithi)- In addition to the common ancestors is the ancestral spirit that acts as the chief overseer of the family. This special guardian's name is revealed by a diviner. A ceremony to incorporate this type of ancestral spirit into the family affairs is also carried out by a diviner. Whenever a family is to embark on a journey or is about to undertake an important task, beer is poured to their shepherd beseeching him for a safety, good health and prosperity.

3. The clan ancestors- Among the clan ancestors, *Kimoi* the founding father of the clan is most revered. Offerings and sacrifices are offered to him. He reciprocates these acts by protecting and assisting the clan members in their various needs. To date, these three spirits are taken seriously especially by elders. Many family misfortunes are associated with lack of harmony between

the family members and the trio hence the need to placate them through sacrifices and rituals. Gehman (1989: 140-142) assigns the following roles to the Akamba ancestors:

a)The living dead are the unseen elders of the family. They function as guardians of the family traditions.

b)When the living members of the family fail to live up to the customs of their fore fathers, it becomes the duty of the ancestors to correct their errors. This correction is more often than not effected through punishment.

c)As elders, the ancestors serve as the owners of the land, fertilizing the earth and causing the food to gr ow. The land becomes sacred since it binds together the living with the ancestors.

d)The living dead receive requests from the living. In this case they act as intercessors for their family members.

e)They serve as intermediaries between the people and God. Since these are still in touch with members of the living community, they are believed to understand human needs better.

f)They act as protectors of the living members of their family. In case of impending danger some ancestors warn members of the living community through dreams. They also protect them from misfortunes. Occasionally, they come to family members with requests of sacrifice or libation of blood, beer or milk.

g)They serve as sources of consolation to the living members of the family who are always conscious of their presence. This comfort comes as a result of the assurance of the constant presence of the ancestors among them especially during the celebration of the various rites of passage.

Ndeti (1972: 118) points out that the living direct their attention to their senior elders who are the living dead in order to maintain unity and harmony among themselves. Because of the role played by ancestors in the family, they are regarded with high esteem. Great care is taken not to offend them. An offense to ancestral spirits is believed to cause problems to the living members of the family such as illness or some kind of misfortune. Harmony between the living and the ancestors is promoted through observation of the norms and regulations of the community, respect, taking into account words pronounced by the ancestors and family elders, invocation of the ancestors, effort by living members to offer constant sacrifices and offerings as required by the community.

Respect of dead members of the family is further expressed through decent funeral rites. For example, if someone dies in a family, it is the role of the family elder to point out the burial site. He does so by digging slightly on the spot even if with a piece of stick or by hand.

To show respect to the departed, the Akamba do not mention their names except during a convocation prayer. They are supposed to be addressed as the departed man or woman, mother, father, sister, brother, girl or boy. It is believed that avoidance of constant mention of their names is an expression of surrender on the part of the living members of the community and, at the same time it enhances the process of their incorporation into the spiritual world.

Observing a careful attention to the words of the ancestors is also very important. Spirits of the living dead may visit family members for various reasons for example, to give a word of wisdom in time of crisis, to make a request or to warn against an impending danger.

Invocation of the ancestors on different occasions such as, embarking on a long journey is yet another way of showing them respect. Ancestors are called upon for protection. During such moments, different ancestors are mentioned by name an indication that they are still in the memory of the living.

Members of the living community endeavor to live up to the norms and regulations of the community to avoid arousing the anger of their ancestors. In this way they dispose themselves to receive blessings and to escape punishment

Sacrifices and offerings are offered to the ancestral spirits from time to time. In the traditional life of the Akamba, families are careful to make libations of beer, milk or water and to give bits of food to the living dead (Lindblom, 1969: 85-86). Each family offers to its ancestors whatever they have of the three drinks at a given time. It is only the father of the home who can offer sacrifice on behalf of his family. He points out that when meat is eaten, fourteen small pieces are offered, if a male relative is visiting, he offers seven pieces. Through the offerings of food, drink and sacrifices, these spirits are kept calm.

Lindblom singles out sacrifice as the most characteristic feature of the conception of *aimu* (spirits) among the Akamba. He notes that, *aimu* are considered to expect constant attention from their living relations, in the form of sacrifice. Although the sacrifice is offered as a gift that the *aimu* need, it is also the channel through which connection with them is maintained and strengthened. Sacrifices, however, are not offered all the time but mainly during moments of crisis, or when something particular is desired and can only be obtained through the help of spirits. Answers to people's needs and requests to the ancestral spirits are sought through the diviner. In some cases however, the ancestors are believed to speak directly to the people. Traditionally, when trouble arose in the family, members avoided speculation by consulting a diviner whose findings were taken for seriously. This tells us why to this day some of the Akamba still believe in what the diviner says about a particular situation or issue.

Veneration of spirits in general

Apart from believing in the living dead, the Akamba recognize the existence of a variety of spirits such as the spirits of water, forests, wind and wandering spirits. Generally spirits are believed to dwell in particular places such as river beds, forests, mountains, hill sides and traditional shrines (Mugambi and Kirima, 1976: 108). They are also believed to occupy the same world as the living.

These anonymous spirits are more feared than the ancestral spirits since they cannot be identified by name. Mugambi and Kirima observed that, some of the spirits experienced by the Akamba were malevolent while others were benevolent. Like the ancestral spirits, all other spirits had sacrifices of animals and offerings of food stuffs offered to them. If not appeased spirits were believed to cause problems to people, through possession, accidents and even sickness among other calamities.

Ways of worship

Sacrifices and offerings- According to Mbiti (1995: 59), the Akamba and Kikuyu make sacrifices on great occasions, such as the rites of passage, planting time, before crops ripen, at the harvest of first fruits, at the ceremony purifying a village after an epidemic and mostly when rains fail or even delay (Mugambi and Kirima, 1976: 59). The Akamba sacrificed oxen, sheep or goats of one colour. An animal of a single color expressed the people's respect of the powerful, pure and glorious God. At times during a serious drought, if animal sacrifice failed, human sacrifice was opted for. Gehman (1989: 203) asserts "After the council of *Kisuka* sacrificed many cows, goats and sheep to no avail, the medicine men said that God wanted to drink human blood. So the Akamba began sacrificing young children, ages 8 to 10" In agreement with Gehman, Mbiti (1995: 59) adds that the child was buried alive in a shrine. This rare sacrifice was offered as the people's highest plea to the highest God for help.

Food offerings were made in thanksgiving to God at harvest time. Up to this day traditional worshipers offer first fruits at the shrines to God before people begin eating fresh food stuffs. Libations of beer, honey, porridge, milk and water were also made. It is believed that if one ate before giving a potion to God this would make God angry and possibly withdraw his blessings.

Prayers and invocations-, Animal sacrifice, food offerings, prayers and invocations were made to God at the shrines for particular intentions. At the shrine, the junior elders slaughtered the goat or the animal of sacrifice. The officiating elder then mixed the blood of the animal with the contents of the stomach and poured at the foot of the tree at the traditional shrine. As the leading elder poured the offering, he would pray to the Creator God saying for instance, *Ngai Mumbi Mwatuangi* (God Creator and divider), we have sacrificed to you so that you can give us rain and food" (Gehman, 1989: 206). Lindblom (1969: 244) records another form of prayer he heard said at child birth: "*Mumbi*, thou who has created all human beings, thou hast conferred a great benefit on us by bringing us this child" Since there was no particular prayer for worship, the officiating elder prayed spontaneously with reference to occasion and purpose.

Traditional worship is further expressed through music and dance especially *Kilumi*. This dance is performed by elderly women and in rare cases elderly men in worship of God and spirits. It is performed on demand in the home of a diviner in response to a particular crisis such as sickness and drought among other personal or communal needs. At the end of each year, this form of worship must be undertaken for three consecutive days reliable to extension. Dances are performed at times to the spirits along side sacrifices and food offerings to appease them. However, if drought persisted, the Akamba then stopped sacrificing to other spirits and turned their attention solely to *Ngai Mumbi* for intervention (Gehman, 1989: 204). Ngai Mumbi is, therefore, the highest God worshiped by the people.

Worship is also expressed through rituals such as the yearly sacrifice of goats by traditional worshipers for common good. The late Ndulili (M.Ndulili, personal communication, March 19, 2008), who was a very strong traditional worshiper told the researcher that at the end of each year, a ritual goat known as *mbui ya muthyuukyo* must be taken round all the villages at night. He said that this is done on the last day of December in the modern calendar. The goat

48

is then sacrificed to God and to all other spirits first, to thank them for their care and protection throughout the year and secondly to implore their blessings for the in-coming year.

Places of worship

We shall view the traditional places of worship under two headings namely; community shrines and family shrines.

Community Shrines- Public worship is always carried out in the community shrines. Sacrifices to the Supreme God and the spirits are offered at the shrines. These are sacred places whereby no one is allowed to tread aimlessly, graze or collect firewood. If one did this, it is counted a disgrace not only to God but to the spirits as well. One day, the researcher and her sister entered a shrine and collected plenty of firewood. On returning home, the first person to meet was a woman diviner in charge of the shrine. On noticing the firewood she immediately commanded that it be returned to the shrine. This was the point at which the researcher understood the sacredness of a traditional shrine. A community shrine could also be erected under a particular tree such as, *mumbu, mukuyu, muamba* and *muumo* (Gehman, 1989: 206) Trees selected for shrines are natural and not planted. Such trees are also huge in size reflecting God's power.

Family shrines- Family shrines were exclusively for family worship. In these shrines sacrifices were offered to God the Creator, to the ancestors and to other spirits such as *ngai sya muviti* (traveling spirits). The family shrine may be a shoot uprooted by the family elder from the community shrine and planted at the grave of an ancestor. Some people use the center post of the house where offerings and libations are poured as a shrine or altar.

Prayer leaders

Among the Akamba, prayer is verbal rather than meditational. The Akamba had no religious priests but the priestly role was performed by two types of elders:

1) *Mutwe*- This being the highest rank of elders, those who attained it have the final say in religious matters. They offer sacrifices to the Creator God. Kitulya Mukala from Kibauni is one among the many surviving elders in this rank. He says that to hold such an office demands that one fully understands the traditions (syithio) of his people and adheres to them without fail lest he offends the spirits.

2) *Syaao*- This is a category lower than that of *mutwe*. They act as assistants to *mutwe* during worship. During the offering of a sacrifice, these elders are responsible for handing over to the chief elder the beer, the meat and the blood at the expected time. Mutune from Ulutya, Matuu belongs to this category of elders.

Although elderly women are allowed to attend shrine worship, they do not play any specific role in the worship and have no particular rank. Normally, the sitting arrangement is in such a way that the two different types of male elders sit separately from women while young men and women sit far off from the altar. The diviner sits with the rest of the men away from the altar. Makula asserted "a diviner is unclean (ni muvuku) and so he cannot sit near the altar or play a significant role in shrine worship" (J. Makula, personal communication, March 29, 2008).

From the discussions done in this chapter, it has surfaced that the traditional

Akamba realized and accomplished their spiritual roles in response to the spiritual world around them through prayer, sacrifices and libations among other practices. In their religious practices, the Akamba were united in one primary intention namely; to maintain a harmonious relationship with the spiritual world and all creation. The Akamba also shared a common belief that, if a good relationship is not maintained between the people and the spiritual world misfortunes would occur. The diviner played a key role in the maintenance of this harmony. For example, if misfortune befell the community such as drought and famine, the elders consulted diviners to establish the cause of this calamity and the way forward. If any form of sacrifice was offered whether on behalf of a family, clan or the entire community, it was because the diviner had been consulted and prescribed it. Although the diviner is not a prayer leader in communal worship, all the same he/she plays a key role in determining what is needed for a ceremony to achieve its goal.

Having presented the traditional experience and practice of religion among the Akamba, it is important at this point to note that, since the event of colonial rule and the coming of missionaries to Kenya, things have not been the same. Today a small fraction of the Akamba has kept faith to traditional ways of worship done by their ancestors. Many people have embraced modern religions, notably, Christianity.

Christianity among the Akamba

The following section presents the contemporary Akamba experience and practice of religion with reference to Christianity which is one of the major religions that has attracted majority of the Akamba. Although Christians do not adhere to traditional ways of worship, in essence, the same God, Creator of the universe is worshiped. Inclusion of this section into the Akamba world view testifies to the fact that society is neither static nor is human thinking. Generally, the Akamba of today have embraced Christianity more than any other religion in the region. Although some people have prescribed to Islam, the number of this portion is quite insignificant. This section will therefore offer a brief view of Christian worship in general since Christianity is not confined to the Kamba community. Special attention is given to the Catholic worship which claims approximately 781,799 adherents in a population of about two million people (Machakos Diocese June, 2003, Episcopal ordination p. 1).

Since the arrival of the missionaries (Baur, 1990: 23) at the Kenyan coast in 1844, Christianity has been accepted, and practiced by majority of the Akamba. In 1851 Krapf visited Ukambani and translated the gospels of Matthew and Mark into Kikamba (Mbula, 1982: 22). According to Baur (1990: 42-44), the African Inland Church entered Kangundo in 1895 and in 1912 the Holy Ghost Fathers also came but later moved to Kabaa and to Kikoko in 1920. The Holy Ghost Fathers (Spiritans) initiated the Catholic Church in Ukambani.

Christian concept of God

It is a bit of challenge for one to define God. This difficulty arises from God's mysterious nature. When Moses dared Him to tell him His name, God simply said "I am who I Am" (Exodus 3: 14). He describes Himself as having been present in the history of His people, yet he continues to be with them forever. God is powerful, loving and caring, merciful, forgiving, everlasting and one who is close to His people from the beginning till the end of all His creation and destiny of humanity. The paradox of God as one in three remains a puzzle to many yet this understanding is the bedrock of Christian faith. God is viewed as a Father, Creator and source of all existence. Jesus Christ, the second person of the Godhead and the incarnate Word of God is the son of God, Savior of the world, the way, the life and the truth (John 4: 25-26, 8: 43, 51). It is the will of the Father that through Him all is drawn to the Father and that by the power of the Holy Spirit, all people will come to the knowledge of the truth (John 16: 13-15). It is to this Triune God that all honour, glory and worship are directed by all who believe.

The Trinitarian concept of God in Christianity is alien to the Akamba traditional concept of God. The God of the Akamba in the traditional setting (Ngai Mumbi Mwatuangi) is far withdrawn from the peoples' day to day lives. In Christianity, intimacy is to be established with the Triune God. Intimacy with God will lead to intimacy and reverence to His creation. For Catholics, reverence to God's angels and saints flows from the understanding that in His love, God shares His power with those He has justified. For this reason they seek the intercession of His angels and saints. Worship, honour and glory are due to God and not to angels and saints. The distinction between the Supreme God who governs all human activity and the beings with which He shares His powers must be made clear to the Christians. Those who subscribe to the powers of a diviner will find it difficult to admit that God is the Supreme power and not the diviner. In this case, although the person may physically go to Church, in the real sense, God is not her/his all in all. Faith in diviners by some Christians can be attributed to the lack of proper understanding of the true nature of God who is the real source of all power. The way diviners present themselves to clients is that they are the sole depositories of the means to penetrate the secrets of the spiritual world. They do so with such confidence that would attract those in crisis situations. One of the diviners interviewed (details ahead) gave this impression to the researcher when she claimed to have a God-given mission to the suffering and needy of society.

Methods of evangelization

To plant the seed of Christianity in Ukambani, the missionaries made use of various techniques. Wherever they settled, missionaries put up a Church, a school and a health center. These three structures still exist in the various parishes of Machakos Diocese such as Kanzalu, Kilungu, Kabaa, Muthetheni, Kasikeu and Mulala among others. Even where a health center did not exist, the missionary sisters for example, The Precious blood Sisters and the Missionary Sisters for Africa operated mobile clinics to far distances. Subsidized charges both in these health centers and in mission schools attracted many to their institutions opening avenues for missionary evangelism. Other methods used were; training of local catechists and doctrinal teaching (Baur, 1990: 68-70). Baptized Christians were at times selected for training as catechists so as to assist in the work of evangelization. The missionaries utilized every possible opportunity to teach the ways of God to the people.

As a method of evangelization, sometimes Christians received free food stuffs and clothing. These offers not only enticed Christians but non-believers too. Perhaps some of the beneficiaries who professed faith in Christ did so, not because they understood His message clearly, but because they wanted to continue receiving material favours from the Church. In one of the parishes where the Missionary Sisters for Africa (from Ireland) worked before handing over to the Little Sisters of St. Francis (an indigenous congregation) more than thirty years a go, the local people still believe that Africans sisters are stingy because they do not supply free clothing, food and free treatment as Sr. Kalla and the rest did. For many years, the community of Kanzalu which is Catholic dominated withdrew from the convent dispensary citing the problem of high treatment charges. This reaction is an indication that some of the methods employed to introduce faith to the people were material oriented and therefore faulty. Although people embraced Christianity, one would wonder whether all those who accepted baptism really understood what it meant to confess faith in Christ. Did they really understand that baptism meant accepting Christ as the Supreme power in their lives or was it simply for material gain? Did they really understand the scope and intensity of the power of God in the universe? If the answer to these questions is 'no', then no wonder today some of the Christians depend on the power of diviners.

In their effort to evangelize the people, missionaries condemned the traditional practices branding them as evil and satanic. Mbula (1982: 31) says "the missionaries looked upon the Africans with great pity; to the extent that Krapf called them 'fallen men from the grace of God, people living in darkness and the shadow of death". These comments were not taken kindly. Even though many were converted to Christianity, not all who viewed the African Cultural practices as evil. According to Mbula, this condemnation has not been effective, hence, the bi-religious attitude experienced today among the Christians. For example, a Christian member of parliament, James Mutiso was mentioned in the weekly Citizen paper (Vol. 9 No. 5 19th -25th December, 2005, p.16) as having drowned in 2003 with a diviner in his car on their way to his home, where she was supposed to prepare a concoction to be served during his electorate party cerebrations.

At times, different missionaries applied methods they felt would best fit their own situations. Perhaps that is why the first white Father in Kasikeu Parish decided to join traditional worshipers in *kilumi* dances in order to talk to them after the dance. He also visited diviners' homes and would sit in sessions for the purpose of understanding the processes. Nevertheless, according to some Christian respondents of this Parish, this strategy did not bear fruit because after a short while, the local people saw no difference between him and them. Without giving room to despair, he tried the use of money to attract the local people to the Parish so as to preach to them. According to some respondents, the priest asked them to dig as many anti-hills as possible and bring them to the Parish. Each anti-hill submitted to the priest was valued for some amount of money. At the end of the day, all the participants gathered under a tree from where the Priest preached to them. This skill later collapsed because some grownups soon felt they were treated like children by being made to bring soil to the Parish.

Without proper evangelization strategies, the Gospel cannot find a home in people's lives. If on the other hand the Gospel does not take root at the time of planting, it is difficult to change anything at a later stage. The researcher casts a critical eye on the manner in which, evangelization was done at the beginning. One wonders why up to this day the diviner is still relevant to Christians.

Types of Christian prayer

Liturgical prayer- This is the official prayer of the Church comprising, the Liturgy of Hours such as Morning Prayer (lauds), Evening prayer (vespers) and Night prayer (compline), and the Eucharist. This description is based on the Catholic understanding of Liturgy. The word Liturgy stands for both the rite of the Eucharist and all rites which make up the common prayer of the Church (Aidan 1991: 182). It is the expression of the Church's deepest point of entry into the mystery of humanity's salvation. It is the prayer of the Church united as a people of God, who continue with the atoning work of Christ. Through the liturgy, the human person steps out of his separateness and becomes a part of the whole; a living organ through which the total message of the Church is expressed and enacted. He views liturgy as a canon of worship in the sense that it instructs its partakers on how to perform their duty. Liturgical prayer follows a particular formula.

Devotional prayer- This type of prayer can be communal or personal. Although the devotions have been allowed by the Church, their practice may be localized to a parish, diocese or country for example, the case of devotion to patron saints. An example of a devotional prayer is the recitation of the Holy Rosary among the Catholics.

Private prayer- This is the personal uplifting of one's mind, heart and soul in praise, honor and adoration to God. In private prayer, there can be no prescribed prayer or formula because this depends on an individual's needs, prayer options, time and place.

The different types of prayers practiced by the Catholics are geared towards personal as well as communal growth in faith. These prayers if not taken with sincerity at a personal level one may remain a nominal Christian though attending services. By talking to different Christians, the researcher noted that most Catholics attend Small Christian Community prayer meetings taking place once a week and the Sunday services only. Not many families pray together every day. Further still, very few people create time for personal prayer. This loophole is an open opportunity for people to lapse back to their traditional ways of life such as consulting diviners caused by lack of personal encounter with the True and Living God.

Ways of Worship

The Liturgy of Hours- This form of worship consists of recitation of psalms and prayers based on the Bible. Although this is a prayer of the Church for all her faithful, it is more known and practiced among the religious and clergy. The congregation for Divine worship (1974: IX) remarks that "The Liturgy of the Hours, which the Church from very early times has been accustomed to recite during the course of the day, she fulfills the command of the Lord to pray without ceasing, and while giving praise to God the Father, at the same time she intercedes for the salvation of the world" Psalms are either recited or sung during prayer.

1. **Celebration of the Eucharist-** On the night before he died, Jesus had his last meal with his disciples. It was during this meal that he took a piece of bread, gave thanks to God, broke it, and gave it to them saying "This is my body which is given for you. "Do this in memory of me" (Luke 22:19). In the same way, he gave them the cup after the supper saying "This cup is God's new covenant sealed with my blood which is poured out for you" (Luke 22: 20).

Three key parts make up the Eucharistic celebration namely: the confessional rite, Liturgy of the word and Holy Communion. In these three steps, the faithful become aware of, and confess their sins in preparation for the holy celebration, they listen to the word of God and finally participate in the commemoration of Christ's death and resurrection after which those fully prepared receive his Body and Blood. By this, the recipients are united with Christ who is truly present, Body and Blood, his self gift to all who believe. It is a celebration of Christ's unlimited love. During the Eucharistic celebration, the faithful offer themselves to God in union with Jesus through bread and wine along side, their farm products and monetary gifts given as an expression of gratitude for God's blessings upon them. On the contrary, during the traditional worship foodstuffs and libations of beer, milk and water offered to God and spirits are not shared by the people. They are a gift given to communicate sincerity of the prayer offered for a particular intention to the spiritual world. The idea of Christ offering Himself to the Father at every Eucharistic celebration as the perfect offering, and giving Himself as food and drink is strange to the Kamba traditional religious thought. Eating together promotes unity. For Catholics receiving the Holy Eucharist means receiving the Body and blood of Christ Himself something that goes beyond a communion meal. Secondly, lack of proper understanding of Christ as the Lamb of sacrifice at each Mass may explain why some Christians accept the diviner's advice to offer a goat to the spirits as a solution to their problems. Incidentally, if such Christians truly believed in the reality of Christ as the perfect offering to God, they would instead request a Priest for a Eucharistic celebration.

Even without partaking of the meal, these gifts which are brought by each family indicate their unity of intention and purpose. In the Catholic celebration, Jesus who is the Lamb of sacrifice gives Himself to the community of worshipers as a gift for their salvation, while at the same time making them one with Him. By His sacrificial death, all who partake of Him are united into His body (Ephesians 2:13). The union achieved through communion with Christ testifies to the union between the individual and the spiritual world.

Figure 1: A Catholic Eucharist procession

Photo by Francis Ng'ang'a
This photo portrays one of the traditional devotions in the Catholic Church.
Under the umbrella is a Priest in the company of other priests, holding the
Blessed Sacrament in a Monstrance. Behind them is a group of
worshippers processing in prayer and adoration. This kind of a ceremony
takes place every year on the feast of the Body and Blood of Jesus Christ .

2. **Singing**- Christian worship is expressed through music and dance. In song

60

we express our feeling of being touched by God's action and our response becomes one of praise, thanksgiving and adoration when it rises up in an expression of our consciousness of salvation. It is a form of worship by which we express our common sense of being touched by God's actions. We praise, adore and glorify God in our worship because He is God in His very self, worthy and deserving all honor and glory from all His creation.

3. **Christian art and symbols in worship-** Art expresses creativity of the human mind. The Catholic Church uses a lot of symbolism in worship especially in form of gestures. In Liturgical dances a lot of gestures are employed such as, lifting of hands during an offertory song and dance to signify self surrender to God and giving back to God the fruits of human labor. Lifting of hands by the priest during the Eucharistic celebration is another example of self surrender. Bread and wine used at each Eucharistic celebration are offered at the altar as symbols of human labor and in turn through the power of the Holy Spirit change into the body and blood of Jesus Christ. At this point they cease to be symbols but a real presence of God Himself. Holy drawings such as, Christ at supper with his disciples, pictures and icons enrich Christian worship too. Union with God can therefore be experienced both individually and communally through the use of material things, symbols, signs, words and actions. In the Akamba traditional religion, art and symbols are an integral part of worship. For example, a long round wooden drum is used during the *kilumi* dances. The wood which is derived from the baobab tree is a symbol of power. The top is covered with an animal skin. The skin is derived from a goat originally offered as a sacrifice by the owner of the drum who is always a diviner. If a diviner happens to convert to Christianity as happened in one of the

outstations in Muthetheni Parish, the drum is either burnt or brought to the Church after its blessing as a sign of the diviner's sincerity. In the view of the researcher, when such a drum is preserved in the Church some people may think that the Church accepts spirit worship as well as the works of diviners unless proper explanation is provided. In fact, this station has a number of cases of people consulting diviners for different purposes.

Participants in worship

Christian worship, both private and liturgical is a continuous act of faith done in appreciation of God's ineffable love and goodness to humanity. It is therefore a universal act of faith; an action of all who believe in Him in union with Christ through the power of His Spirit. Prayer leaders are both ordained ministers and lay baptized Christians. In the Catholic Church, all other forms of worship can be carried out by any one ordained or not, except the celebration of the Eucharist which is exclusively the duty of an ordained priest.

When worship takes place

Private prayer can be done at any time and at any place conducive to prayer whenever one wants to be united with his/her Creator. Liturgical prayer however is celebrated at particular times for example, the divine office in the morning, evening and at night. The Eucharist can be celebrated on daily basis but "Sunday is the official day for the liturgical assembly, when the faithful gather to listen to the word of God and take part in the Eucharist, calling to mind the passion, resurrection, and glory of the Lord Jesus" (Catechism of the Catholic Church, 1995: 305). The Liturgical celebration runs according to the calendar of the Church with two major seasons; Christmas and Easter. Within the liturgical year, there are other feasts and solemnities observed such as those of the Blessed Virgin Mary and the Saints.

Where worship takes place

Liturgical worship can be carried out in any place set aside for this purpose. However, in the celebration of the Eucharist, a Church is used in which an altar is erected. Where need arises, the Eucharist can also be celebrated outside a Church but in a well set ground.

Disposition during worship

Christian worship is carried out in an atmosphere of silence and re-collective mood. This kind of disposition enables the worshiper to become composed, discarding roaming desires and elevating concentration on that thing alone which, for the time being is the only one that matters (Guardini, 1963: 16).

Conclusion

Contact with the Akamba historico-socio-religious background leads to the realization that they are a people who have a concrete background and culture. Their history and geography testifies to their unity as a community. They have remained in their ancestral land to this day with an exception of few who have migrated to other places. As a community, they have continued to experience life together something that has, to a given extent, enabled them to keep to their traditional beliefs and practices. Although much has eroded away, this rich heredity is still experienced in different ways and in varied intensities.

This chapter has emphasized the current practice of traditional religion among the Akamba which includes the practice of divination. It has emerged clearly that, although Christianity has largely spread among the Akamba, it has not completely annihilated traditional beliefs and practices among the people. For example, in October 21, 2007 a neighbour who happened to be a confessed Christian had a quarrel with his brother after which his child got involved in a car accident. This accident was immediately attributed to witchcraft. Interpretation of this incident confirmed to the researcher that traditional religion still influenced the Akamba social and spiritual lives. Members of this same family turned against one another two years later (2009) and demanded that one of them be taken to a ritual diviner to have his witchcraft powers neutralized. Owing to this reality we realize that, although some Akamba Catholic Christians attend Church services, commune with the rest of the Christians and appear to be fully one with the Church, they are indeed immersed in their traditional beliefs and practices. This dilemma underlies the purpose of this study namely to find out why such Christians believe that in time of turmoil, a diviner is the answer and not Christ.

CHAPTER THREE: THE UNIVERSALITY OF THE INSTITUTION OF DIVINERS

Introduction

This chapter is highly instrumental to the study. It focuses on what other scholars have written on diviners. It views the broader concept and role of diviners in various African communities as well as communities outside Africa. Areas related to the problem under study have been identified as follows: The African concept of a diviner, experience of a diviner in African communities, becoming a diviner, types of diviners, the motive of the institution of diviners, diviners worldwide, diviners in the Bible, the response of the Catholic Church in Machakos to the menace of diviners, gospel and culture, levels of culture and inculturation. The chapter closes with a brief conclusion.

The African concept of a diviner

This section answers two fundamental questions namely; what is the African concept of a diviner? What role does he/she accomplish in society? The two questions will be treated simultaneously.

There is a vast variation in the understanding of who a diviner is in Africa. This can be seen in the different studies carried out by different scholars in different places and time. For example, Olupona (2000:87) describes a diviner as one who stands in the crossroads between the physical and the spiritual world as an intercessor and mediator who bridges communication between the two worlds. Diviners according to him explore and exploit the mystical world to normalize, ameliorate, restore and reconcile estranged relationships for a harmonious and habitable universe.

Tempels (1969: 86) adds to the understanding of a diviner in his ethnographic study carried out among the Baluba people of Congo. The purpose of his study was the search of Bantu philosophy. Tempels describes a diviner (nganga or kilumbu) as a man who possesses a clearer than usual vision of natural forces and their interaction, the man who has the power of selecting these forces and of directing them towards a deterministic usage in particular cases. He adds that, such a man is what he is only because he has been seized by the living influence of a deceased ancestor or of a spirit.

By engaging in long discourses with the people and spending time observing them, Placide discovered that anomaly, defect and illness are linked in some way to evil. To counteract these evils, purificatory practices, rites, prohibitions and ablutions were carried out. In his study, he established that the key aim behind all these practices among the Bantu is either to protect or to increase the vital force (Tempels 1969: 175). He also discovered that, behind these practices was the diviner who acted as a discerner. For example, a diviner is brought in to decide whether an illness or a misfortune that has supervened in the interval following the demise of the deceased should be blamed on him or not, and whether the deceased is to be regarded as friendly or hostile. If his life brought distress to the clan or to strangers his spirit will be regarded as hostile unlike the spirit of a person who in his life time exhibited peace (Tempels, 1969: 157-158). Tempels continues to assert that in case of undesirable incidents such as accidents, illness or even death the Baluba will not rush to infantile judgment of the deceased person. Instead, the intermediary or a diviner is sought to table the one behind it.

66

Akiiki (1982: 73) observes that diviners are believed to be extraordinary people whose vocation is the result of a special favour from the spirit-world. In some societies they number among the mystics who are believed to be betrothed to the divinities they serve. Before assuming their responsibilities they are given a special training. Through these rituals they are declared the "Spouse" of the divinity, capable of entering into mystical union with the spirit-world.

Turner (1967:42) describes diviners as persons who use medicinal powers particularly supra normal powers, in favor of life. He notes that among the Sukuma of Tanzania diviners apply various skills to meet the medical needs of the community.

All the above scholars mentioned seem to agree that a diviner is one who stands out in the community with special ability to unveil some esoteric knowledge to his/her clients. From the above discussions we realize that Africans share a common understanding of diviners and that they place them at a level higher than that of the rest in the community. This view is very significant to this study. More often than not, the concept one has about something determines his/her relationship with it. In this study, information was sought regarding the Akamba concept of a diviner in a bid to explain why people of different status as well as Christians particularly Catholics find value in the diviner. Christianity for example, preaches faith in the power of God, the Supreme force behind all existence. When Christians ignore this reality and present their problems to a diviner, it raises many questions on their understanding of the Christian faith that need to be carefully addressed. These scholars also place a lot of emphasis on diviners as people who act at the impulse of some spirits. This being the case, knowledge of the kind of spirits that control the Akamba diviners was necessary to provide answers to some of the questions underlying this study such as "how does the contemporary Akamba community view diviners?

Becoming a diviner in Africa

Becoming a diviner among the Africans is quite a challenge and because of this, not all who desire to be can achieve this goal. Diviners view their service in the community as a call from ancestors or superhuman powers. Their choice according to Turner (1975: 247-249) is manifested through some irregular behaviours, illness or misfortune. Suspicions about such symptoms are confirmed through divination. It is believed that if this call is not responded to correctly insanity or even more serious repercussions may befall the intended candidate. Morris (1976: 243) adds that, for one to be accepted for training as a diviner, he/she must portray certain characteristics such as high intelligence, good memory and personal control. Ngong Njia (2004:64) cites further requirements by asserting that such people must be men and women whose main purpose is to promote life force either by healing or by nullifying evil in society. Secondly, they must be tested publicly in the diagnostic skills and spiritual powers of divination art to ascertain that they can 'sniff out' the secrets of the underworld and unearth the truth in the community.

Among the Zulu people of South Africa a candidate begins by becoming "delicate", abhorring certain foods, telling of his constant dreams, abstaining from various things and constantly complaining of pains in different parts of the body. Eventually, the candidate falls ill. This necessitates the intervention

68

of a diviner. If the candidate is destined to become a diviner he/she tells the family members who keep watch for further signs. Due to the ambiguity of these signs, it may take long to bring the person round. The person finally requests the family not to give him/her any more medicines. With time he/she begins to manifest real signs of a diviner through his/her illness. He yawns again and again, becomes fond of snuff, cries aloud, gets convulsions, leaps like a frog and his body shakes violently, and keeps people awake by singing songs that further confirm his future mission (Gallaway, 'in Peek, 1991:23-24). According to Gallaway, this most devastating situation may be brought to an end by a spirit that visits him in the night and commands him to visit a certain diviner for cleansing as well as carrying out other necessary rituals. Confirmation is only actualized at the onset of his career when the spirits begin speaking through him during a divination process. In case the family of this new candidate does not wish their son to become a diviner, they are free to invite a doctor to lay off the spirit in possession of him.

Gallaway further cites the case of the Yaka of Zaire the current Democratic Republic of Congo. According to him, for one to be accepted to the diviners' institution, symptoms similar to those of a Zulu candidate should manifest. Candidates at times manifest some peculiarities such as depression, persistent illness, nausea, dysmenorrhea, headache, suffocation, stiffening and itching. Other symptoms are convulsions, jumping high up while in a state of trance or climbing a tree suddenly. The candidate may begin to see appearances of other deceased diviners, feel feverish and experience a lot of fear of being wounded or loosing a lot of blood (for hunters). Among the Yaka, diviners take a period of nine months to be initiated into their ministry. Just as a foetus remains in the mother's womb for nine months in the same way does a Yaka diviner remain a neophyte. At the end of the nine months, the initiate is born into a new ministry and can now operate independently. One only experiences full health after the initiation process has been completed. Among the Yoruba, there are formal schools where diviners are trained. Complete training takes a period of 10 Years during which the *Ifa* divination knowledge is keenly passed on (Abimbola, 1967: 110).

Turner, Gallaway and Abimbola are in agreement that for one to become a diviner, some symptoms must precede. However, from some discussion with one of the Akamba diviners (M. Ndulili, personal communication, March 19, 2008), the researcher learned that this is not always the case among the Akamba diviners. For Ndulili, he simply admired the healing ministry after which he took a personal initiative to visit a diviner who practiced within his area of interest. He was then asked to give to his trainer a bull and later during inauguration to offer some other animal sacrifice. This indicates that there are no uniformed pointers to the diviners' career in Africa.

In harmony with Mukanda's case, Tempels (1969) notes that among the Baluba, the person who desires initiation into divination must take the initiative of requesting for training as prove of his/her conviction. Tempels contends that "nganga" can only teach his apprentice the different manipulations and ceremonies of his art and train him in the behaviour he ought to adopt in the higher life for which he is intended. However, he warns that it does not lie within his power to give force or knowledge to a candidate (1969:87). It therefore means that the training diviner can only expose a candidate to the means of acquiring this power but not to empower him/her in reality as this is the work of the spirits. From these discussions, it emerges that spirits play a key role in the life of a diviner.

Citing the case of the Yoruba people of West Africa, Mbiti (1995:233) maintains that training of diviners is done privately by other diviners which gives the new initiates an opportunity to work as apprentices for three to seven years. In this case, divination is learned more through practice than by formal training. Likewise, Akiiki (1982:73) concurs with his fellow scholars in their view that diviners undergo special rituals to consecrate themselves to the new state of life. In support of the need for training, this study views the formal and practical training that new diviners are subjected to before confirmation to their ministry, as one of the tools that elevate them above the rest of the community members. Training and practice therefore are the gate ways to perfection in divination.

In this section, it has emerged that diviners must undergo some kind of training to be accepted as societal specialists. In most African countries there was no collective training of new practitioners as already implied in the preceding discussions. For example, in the case of Yoruba diviners of West Africa, training was done privately and through experience. Although this approach has been applied for many years among the Yoruba, this researcher points to its possible weakness that, while the training diviner passes on his/her skills to the other, he/she could also pass on his/her limitations hence weakening the institution. Depending on one's personality, one may for one reason or another be unwilling to reveal certain skills to the neophyte. Perhaps this may explain why some diviners may be more skilled than others. More about diviners and their areas of specialization will be treated in the next section.

Types of diviners

Diviners are of different types. They are classified either by the roles they play or the instruments used. Different diviners use tools related to the nature of their call. For example, among the Nandi of Kenya, there are four kinds of diviners based on the role they play in the community. They are Kipsakeiyot and Kipngut who deal with spirits of the dead and Sakeiyuot and Orkoiyot who are witch-doctors (Mbula, 1982:112). In our study, we shall take into consideration three major categories based on the nature of roles played by each group namely; instrumental/mechanical diviners, mediumistic/spirit and augury diviners.

Instrumental/mechanical/diagnostic diviners

This category of diviners presents the most common type of divination across the continent. It covers a wide range of divination tools as here discussed:

1) **Book diviners-** This type of diviners accomplish their divination task by examining Arabic books. It employs techniques such as counting of numbers, measurements, the divination of time as measured by clock, writing and reading certain verses. This type of divination was first applied by Muslims to determine and solve cases brought to them ((Peek, 1991:160). To this type of diviners time is very important. Yahaya a renowned diviner in Bunyole Uganda said "my science is that of the seven days, I know how every hour is called and what can be done at that time" According to him, by use of this approach he is able to determine the kind of a person behind the client's trouble, where medicine was buried, and the type of sacrifice needed for the cure. Besides the use of an authoritative book, clients of *Lamuli* diviners claimed that these practitioners were able to find out the truth without the help of spirits.

2) In Bunyoro, diviners use strips of leather, wooden charms, grains or rubbing stick. Nupe diviners make use of cowry shells and palm nuts or Tortoise shells (Peek 1991: 165) Both Mbiti (1995:232- 233) and Bascom ("in Magesa, 1998:198) agree that the Yoruba diviners make use of *Ifa* divination in which sixteen palm nuts are manipulated or a divining chain is cast. Casting of the chain involves the use of sixteen cowries. Both methods involve a specialized knowledge of divining verses that are both difficult and time consuming to learn. Diviners are trained on how to read and interpret the palm nuts or cowries that have been tossed to the ground. Training also involves learning of names and signs of divination figures, the proverbs and stories connected with them. Mbiti further asserts that divination can also be done through the use of stones, gourds, palm reading, form or seeing images in pots of water, interpreting animal marks, listening to and interpreting sounds and using séances by means of which the diviner gets in touch with the spirit world. The Ndembu of Zambia divine by use of a divination basket, by rattle, by calabash, bush back horn, stick bundle and tortoise shells (Turner, 1975). Among the Agikuyu of Kenya, a small bell (rogambi) was used by diviners (Kenyatta, 1978:291).

The variety of tools used by different diviners is an indication that diviners do not use the same tools. Although generally they deal with dilemmas in human life, each diviner is localized hence making use of those symbols and items familiar to his/her society. Without discovering the tools used by the Akamba diviners this study would not be complete. This study established that the Akamba diviners use more less the same type of tools. These tools are unique in themselves as they seem to invoke in clients the feeling of a mysterious presence. By the manner in which they manipulate their tools, diviners attract more and more clients to themselves who visit in hope of having their problems solved.

Augury oracular divination

Pritchard (1977: 258-386) in his study of the Azande employed observer participatory approach over a long period of time. His purpose was to understand their religion. After his study he reported that the oracular type of divination is common among the Azande and it involves observing a selected animal, dead or alive. The behaviour of a live animal or some feature of a dead one enables the diviner to augur what is in store for the waiting client.

Magesa (1997:200) identifies two types of augury form of divination, the poison oracle and the "bad signs" The poison oracle involves the introduction of poison derived from a special plant known as *benge* into a live animal, preferably a fowl. This procedure brings together three people namely the client (the owner of the fowl), the one who operates and introduces the poison and the questioner. The questioner says "If such is the case, poison kill the fowl, or if such is the case, poison spare the fowl. The verdict according to Magesa depends on whether the fowl dies or not. A practical example would be: "If K has committed murder poison, kill the fowl and if K is innocent poison spare the fowl". If the fowl dies, poison is induced into a second fowl. To the second fowl the questioner will say "the poison oracle has declared K guilty of murder by killing the fowl. If it is true that K is guilty let the poison spare the fowl. If the fowl survives, then K is guilty. If the results are contradictory then they are invalid. Observation involves taking note of the fowl's behavior while under the oracle that is, how the poison affects it. In

74

questioning, one must be well experienced to know whether to pose a positive or a negative question. For an accurate judgment, if the first fowl dies a second fowl must survive the second test and vise versa. Magesa says that, in the second type of poison oracle some vital part of the client is brought into contact with parts of animals killed for the divination purpose. Some part of an animal such as, the liver is examined for any bad sign. This type of divination is common among the Banyoro of Uganda.

The bad sign type of divination according to the researcher can be risky in that inexperienced diviners may ask the animal a negative question instead of a positive one hence tampering with the outcomes. This same risk can also be found in the mechanical type of divination. All this raises questions on the authenticity of the diviner's message to a client an area not treated by any of these scholars. The study therefore puts into consideration the question of acceptance of the diviner's message as true or doubtful.

Mediumistic / spirit diviners

These diviners operate under the influence of one or more spirits. In most cases, the spirits may be of deceased family members or of other departed diviners. Among the Nyole the spirits may come from one's uncles. Although most mediums are women, mediumistic divination is practiced by both men and women. Some scholars however, argue that women practice mediumistic roles because other avenues are denied them. On the contrary, Shaw and others (Peek, 1991:133) view women mediums as serving a special call and superior in position that enables them to become the channels of revelation during divination.

Citing the case of the Lulua, Basonge and the Baluba of Congo, Zahan (1979: 83-84) comments that a diviner is always an intermediary between the souls of the dead and his clients, the living. Among the Nyole, some diviners seemed to conceive of their relationship with their spirits as similar to marriage. Reinolds (in Peek 1991: 158) refers to some two women who mentioned to her that their spirits were like their husbands; they had to sleep in the *amasawo* with them. A mediumistic diviner works in association with another diviner to interpret the message delivered through him/her since he/she does not know at the moment of possession what is taking place (Mugambi & Kirima 1976:76). Mbiti (1992:172) concurs with Mugambi and Kirima and adds that, the medium working with the diviner thrusts out information on the cause, nature and treatment of a disease while the diviner follows or interprets the instructions from the medium. Out of experience, the researcher is in agreement with the claims of these scholars. I had the opportunity of watching a *kilumi* dance during which a woman diviner went into trance and began speaking profusely, jumping up and down and at times stepping on fire until another diviner in the dance began shaking hands with her, inquiring from the spirit what it needed. After a long conversation the interpreter said "if it is just a sacrifice you need, it will be provided" At these words the possessed diviner became calm but fatigued.

Mediumistic divination can be a challenging procedure due to its complexity. One wonders whether in the fast flowing words of the medium the interpreter could not miss out some necessary details hence affecting both efficiency and effectiveness of the session prescriptions. The above information on diviners reveals that they differ from each other both in charisma and in the tools they use to accomplish their role in society. Africans treat this not as a point of conflict but as a complementary reality hence a welcome existence. In the study of the Akamba diviners, it was established that they used different instruments. The intention here was to ascertain whether these differences contributed in any way to clients' attraction to diviners.

Having examined the different forms of diviners in Africa, the next section will explore the purpose for which diviners actually exist in society.

The practice of divination in Africa

Parrinder (1962: 103) in his study of religious beliefs in Africa gathered material from various parts of the continent and in particular, Africa south of Sahara the area stretching from Sierra Leone in the west to the Nuba mountains in the east, and down to the Cape in the south. He conducted a field study using the comparative approach to analyze data. In his report, he identifies four types of sacred specialists namely: priests, mediums, diviners, herbalists and witch-doctors. Parrinder describes an African diviner as a specialist who seeks to diagnose disease, or discover the solution to problems, by means of inspiration or manipulation of objects through various techniques. The researcher concurs with Parrinder that there is a close link between mediums, priests and diviners. His observation that some diviners may be subject to spirit possession and give their answers by recourse to an oracle was revealed to the researcher by some diviners as a common phenomenon among diviners. This reveals the esoterical character of diviners in which their career is seen to be nearer to the spiritual realm than the material. This character adds value to diviners leading people to consult them with hope of receiving a higher form of solution to their problems.

Another yet fascinating study was carried out by Tempels (1969) among the Baluba people of Congo. His main concern was the understanding of Bantu philosophy. A comparative approach was adopted in the study of modes of behavior, languages, institutions and customs (1969:41-44). The conclusions of this study were that Bantu behavior is centered on a single value: vital force. Vital force is life force or living strongly. In his study, Tempels established that, when the Bantu visit a diviner the purpose is to learn the words of life and the way of making life stronger. The diviner in this case is viewed as a superior human force as compared to the rest of the people. The researcher agrees with Tempels that all human beings desire to live strongly. The sustenance of this vital force is what brings challenges to the people according to him. Tempel's observation is quite relevant to this study in that it sheds light into the question of the relevance of diviners to contemporary Akamba community. It challenges the researcher to dig deeper into that which attracts the Akamba of today to the diviner. For example, Tempels observed that among the Bantu the diviner is seen as a superior human force. This view applies very closely to that of the Akamba who consult the diviner when all else has failed. This is because he/she is thought to possess some extra-ordinary ability to unveil hidden secrets.

Zahan (1978:82) observes that diviners in the African community are believed to possess special abilities that enable them to act as mediators between the living and the spirit world. Given the various roles that they accomplish, they are revered as restorers of community harmony especially where suspicion, anger and hatred among other vices may have brought division. In most cases, this harmony is enabled through rituals. In this sense Kalilombe observes that the outcome of the project of life depends on how successful and beneficial the relationships are between the living and the invisible world. Diviners are therefore needed by the Africans to ensure that community harmony is maintained.

Belief in diviners and the practice of divination is to be found in the Christian realm too. Studies have shown that this is a common phenomenon in the human society. For example, Gehman (1989: 98) refers to Ronald Regan's reliance on astrology for his schedules and plans during his tenure of office. Both the President and the First Lady then are said to have been quite superstitious, observing rituals as knocking on wood and walking around and not under ladders and putting on a lucky gold charm in their pockets every morning. Gehman comments that although the president seems to have a deep Christian faith, he seems untroubled by the contradictions of depending on the mystical powers of astrology even while professing faith in Christ and the Gospel. The expression "deep Christian faith" by Gehman does raise a lot of questions. In the opinion of this researcher, to have deep Christian faith is to be wholly devoted to the teachings and the values of Christ. Nevertheless, he does put it well that, the life of this Christian was coupled with contradictions. The question is, "Are there Regans in the Catholic Church today?

Among the Kiga people of Kabale diocese in Uganda, a research key to this study was carried out by Kaheeru (1990). The study aimed at examining the people's traditional practices of medicine and healing in the light of Christ's healing ministry in Luke. The study was based on survey design. The main instrument of data collection was questionnaires that were distributed to 120 people. The researcher also held interviews with some of his key informants. In his report diviners emerge as specialists in diagnosing causes of day to day problems among the people. This specialist role is the one that attracts people to diviners in this Diocese. Although Kaheeru made inquiry among the laity, he does not specify the kind of specialists he approached for information. The study among the Akamba of Ikalaasa, Ekalakala and Kasikeu made enquiries among the diviners themselves and about the roles they accomplish in society.

Another study carried out by Mwendwa (1990) among the Akamba of Kitui sought to investigate the healing ministry of Christ with reference to the traditional healing practices of the Akamba. He used survey design leading to field study in which interviews were conducted. His findings were that the Kamba traditional healer is charismatic, prophetic and a diviner. Diviners according to this study underwent a special initiation rite (kukunulwa uwe) during which they received divination tools of a calabash (kititi) with seeds (mbuu), a musical bow (uta), chalk (ia) and herbs for healing (miti). Diviners among these people seek to investigate the cause of evil or sickness and its cure through their knowledge and wisdom of ancestors. This study saw the healing ministry of Christ as continued among the people of Kitui through the diviner. The current study experiences some difficulty with this view. While the diviner is well accepted as a healer in the traditional society, the researcher raises questions on the source of diviners' power to heal. Chapters five and six will do some follow up on this.

Further study on divination was carried out by David McLean and Ted Solomon (In Peek, 1991:69-71) among the Bena Lulua people. Their basic argument was that divination was not only a basic pattern in understanding the Lulua way of life but that it was also the most important institution in this society. The study emphasizes divination's centrality in articulating culture and providing sufficient knowledge for orderly, meaningful human existence. They continue to argue that contrary to previous assertions that divination is merely supportive of kinship and political structures, closer examination reveals that a divination system involves far more than religious belief. It is necessary in providing a repository of cultural values as well as facilitating adjustments to a changing society. As a point of emphasis, the study points out that the practice of divination requires the reunification of social units through collective recounting of personal and group history as well as reviewing behavioral standards in light of a contemporary dilemma. The case of the Bena Lulua people unearths a fundamental point in the question of preservation of cultural values. According to Mbiti (1995: 178) diviners express these community values as counselors, judges, comforters, suppliers of assurance and confidence during people's crises, advisors, seers, priests and pastors. By performing these roles, they constantly draw people back to their beliefs, practices and values. Nevertheless, both of these studies do not address the exact issues that the Akamba diviners deal with such as witchcraft and healing. These gaps form the main content for discussion in chapter five.

Among the Batammaliba of Togo (in Peek 1991:73), a very interesting study in relation to diviners' ministry was carried out by Rudolph Blier. The researcher focused on the social dimensions of the people's medical care and how they viewed, defined, categorized and treated health related crisis. The outcomes of the study were that diviners among the Batammaliba served as pastoral guides, consultants, and redefining, re-explaining and reinterpreting cultural elements of the people. These observations tally with those of Mbiti, Maclean and Solomon in their view of divination as a means of enhancing the people's cultural values. In chapter three of this dissertation (3.9), it was pointed out that diviners among the Akamba play the role of resolving family and clan conflicts resulting from witchcraft claims. In most cases, the Akamba resolve this conflict by forcing both the suspect and all married members of the family or clan to undergo a witchcraft eradication ritual. For quite some time now this has been one of the greatest challenges facing the Catholic Diocese of Machakos.

A study carried out in Madagascar among the Antemoro by Pierre Verin and Narivelo Rajaonarimanana ('in Peek, 1991:53) aimed at providing a synthesis of previous contributions as well as devising a new approach to understanding the divination system. Through interaction and holding both formal and informal inquiries among the people, these researchers were able to establish that these people considered diviners with vitality due to their esteemed roles in the society. Diviners in Madagascar act as counselors, judges, comforters, suppliers of assurance and confidence in moments of crisis; advisors, priests, seers, fortune tellers, and revealers of secrets such as theft or imminent danger. The study further established that although divination as well as the idol cults had been said to be disappearing from the realm of acceptable beliefs among these people, nevertheless, divination practices are still in use, not only in the pagan coastal areas but also in the very heart of Imerina and Betsileo country. The *Ombiasy* (diviner) according to them relies on astrology for example, to define favorable and unfavorable days and therefore recommends the proper procedures to be followed so that the client achieves the desired results for the day. These diviners are believed to possess esoteric knowledge. The study revealed the diviner as one who plays integral roles in the community of Antemoro of Madagascar. The current study endeavored to inquire from the Akamba diviners and their clients, the role played by diviners in the community. This inquiry was viable in guiding the researcher to articulate clearly the diviners' role among the Akamba observable in chapter five. In view of the reality of diviners in Madagascar, this study sought to establish the extent to which the Catholics of Machakos Diocese are involved with divination practices.

Among the Yoruba of Nigeria, a study by Osunwole (1991: 77) reveals the diviner as one who is concerned with saving lives rather than causing misfortune. Osunwole's observation is in agreement with Tempels (1969) in his view that the diviner among the Baluba is one who concerns himself with the promotion of the people's vital force. Among the Yoruba, a diviner is referred to as the father of mysteries. To be able to detect the root cause of a problem, various diviners in this community make use of *Ifa* divination. He is one with great intellectual capabilities, intuition and possesses the facility for probing the universe and to interpret its responses. By this, the diviner is able to come up with answers to the client's problems. Yoruba diviners have power over witches and, through rituals, can compel a witch to confess her wicked ways (Osunwole, 1991:78). The Akamba diviners play a similar role hence the reason why many Christians fall back to them.

Mbiti (1995: 177) presents various studies done in different African communities. In his findings he draws a difference between a medicine man/woman and a diviner. According to him a medicine man/woman deals purely with herbal medicines while a diviner is more concerned with diagnosis and prescriptions. While Mbiti's findings apply correctly to the Akamba situation, the researcher charges that some diviners go beyond diagnosis and prescriptions and assume the role of healers. Observations by the researcher of a woman diviner *Syosala* who died in 1987, were that she diagnosed, prescribed and provided some herbal treatment to some clients. At the level of discussion of findings, this study sheds more light on the role played by diviners among the Akamba.

Mbiti (1995: 177) further describes diviners as agents of unveiling mysteries of human life. Divination according to him is generally done through the use of mediums, oracles, being possessed, divination objects, common sense, intuitive knowledge and insight, hypnotism, and other secret knowledge. He observes that in order to accomplish their role, Yoruba diviners particularly make use of the *Ifa* system which deals with figures and complications of numbers among other complicated applications. Mbiti (1995: 178) further acknowledges that, divination is done by use of various methods such as pebbles, numbers, water, animal entrails, reading the palm and by throwing dice among many others. According to him most African diviners do not undergo prolonged formal training such as those found among the Yoruba and a few other West African communities. In his study, he noted a mediumistic role in the practice of divination. He mentions that mediums link human beings with the living dead and the spirits who either play the role of a diviner or work together with him/her in the divination process (1995: 170). Most important in his findings was that in divination there is a certain amount of communication that proceeds between diviners and non human powers as well as the diviner's extra sensory ability, spiritual agents, telepathy, sharpened human perception or combination of all the possibilities. The diviner fulfills an intermediary function between the physical and the psychical and between the human and spiritual during a divination session.

Unlike other scholars, Mbiti shows that a diviner is an ordinary human person but one who at times accomplishes his divination role through the help of spirits and some other extra-ordinary virtues. He, however, agrees with them that a diviner is an intermediary between the human and the spiritual. At a deeper level, all the scholars so far mentioned are in agreement that a diviner is an integral healer of society. This discovery posed a challenge to the researcher to investigate further on what an integral Kamba diviner does in the community.

A study by Ngundo (1999) carried out in Muthetheni Parish sought to establish the impact of the belief in witchcraft on Christians. A hundred and fifty people participated in the study. Analysis of the data collected revealed that many Akamba believed in the reality of witchcraft. As a result of this belief, the study established that the people's faith was duly affected leading them to live in suspicion, fear of one another and even fear of attending small Christian community prayer with some suspect witches. Although the researcher was able to establish the reality of the belief in witchcraft among the Akamba, she does not tell us what people do in order to deal with the consequences of this belief. The current study is built on observations that, when confronted with the problem of witchcraft and other dilemmas of life, some people consult a diviner in search of a solution.

A study carried out by Olupona in the year 2000 on the Chadic speaking groups of eastern and south eastern Jos Plateau in Nigeria, focused on the ritual frame work of *Pa* divination as an indicator of ritual time and places. To collect data, participant observer methods were applied as well as interviews. The study especially dealt with the area of individual affliction, conflict and crises caused by spiritual human agents. Findings of the study were that *Pa* means to cover something. It is therefore that form of divination that deals with that which is hidden and secret (Olupona, 2000:88). Secrets are revealed by casting pebbles. The study further notes that, *Pa* divination is a mechanism through which social conflicts are excluded and resolved and that, rituals are performed in case of crisis and breach of regular norms governing relationships in human society. When Olupona makes reference to afflictions caused by spiritual human agents, it is not clear whether these are spirits or humans per se. Further still, his study ignores afflictions that can be caused by forces other than human agents such as madness resulting from spirit possession yet these are part and parcel of afflictions in human life. One wonders how the diviner isolates one from the other. The current study examines different methods used by the Akamba diviners in dealing with various human afflictions.

A study carried out by Kasomo among the Akamba sought to examine the effect of the belief in mystical powers on the lives of the Akamba Catholics of Tawa parish, Makueni County (2000). The study established that in this parish there was evident belief in mystical powers such as magic and witchcraft. While his major concern was the effect of the belief in mystical powers on the lives of the Akamba Catholics, the current study is concerned with the relevance of diviners in contemporary Kamba community something that does not feature in his study.

Another study carried out among the Akamba was by Munuve (2001). His study was a search on the phenomenology of *Masya/Ngata* ritual as a witchcraft eradicator and deterrent among the Akamba. Respondents were drawn from Kitui, Machakos and Makueni counties. The study was motivated by a wave of oath taking that had hit these areas. In his study he established the reality of the people's participation in traditional oaths (Christians inclusive), mode of operation and the beliefs underlying the act. A traditional specialist in rituals administered the oaths.

Munuve's study revolved around 'ngata' (traditional oaths). His study was geared towards establishing whether or not people actually participated in these rituals. He also sought to understand the nature of these rituals and their purpose. Although his findings inform this study on a particular traditional oath used as witchcraft eradicator among the Akamba, it only focuses on one type of a diviner and his role in the community. The current study views Akamba diviners as being more than ritual specialists.

Another fascinating study conducted by the Cultural Research Center, Jinja (2003) dwelt on the topic; "Witchcraft, Divination and Healing among the Basoga". Different research assistants carried out field investigations mainly through questionnaires and interviews. The findings of the study were that, divination among the Basoga is practiced as a means to counteract the forces of evil. It is the traditional means of diagnosing the root cause of a problem. The views of this study link closely to those of Temples among the Baluba people. According to the Basoga, a diviner is capable of learning and telling his clients about the past, the present and future as well as offering solutions to their problems either in the form of herbs or psychological and spiritual counseling. These people believe that the diviner's power is chiefly from spirits as well as the medicines used. Although the study among the Basoga highlights on the purpose of divination among these people, it does not address the methods used in diagnosing a problem. This knowledge gap has been taken care of in the current study in its examination of the different methods used by the Akamba diviners.

Another case at hand is that of the Akamba Catholics of Mwala. Kasomo (2003) carried out a study among these people to establish the nature, causes and participation in traditional oathing. He did a survey study in which he distributed questionnaires to more than 600 people. The results of his study were that the Akamba of this area participated in traditional oaths as a means of resolving witchcraft related conflicts among them. At the center of these rituals was the diviner whom he describes as a very skillful cult urologist and psychoanalyst who is always familiar with arts and knowledge of social deities. The diviner according to the results of this study annuls curses inflicted to individuals through traditional oaths. The ritual is aimed at restoring peace among those affected. He accomplishes this by the use of magical medicine (muthea). The study by Kasomo examined one role of a diviner among the Akamba. The current study explores more deeply the various roles played by diviners today in view of establishing their relevance to the Akamba of the Catholic Diocese of Machakos. Unlike the quantitative approach used by Kasomo, this study used a qualitative approach for the purpose of acquiring detailed information on the people's experiences with diviners.

Further study on diviners was carried out among the Baganda of Uganda by Ssegawa (2004) on the topic; Sickness among the Baganda of Uganda; A pastoral Care of the Sick. Like Kaheeru (1990) this study established that diviners play a big role in the treatment of sickness, in unveiling secrets and informing people about the causes of their problems. To accomplish their roles, diviners use the chicken method, coffee berries, leather throw method and the water test method. To study the above phenomena among the Christians, Ssegawa applied the pastoral method of insertion, social analysis and theological reflection. On the contrary, the current researcher employed the phenomenological approach which enabled her to study designated phenomena in their natural settings. Although these studies bring the diviner to the center of the healing ministry, they do not specify whether both Christians and non Christians acknowledge the diviner as their healer. As a step further, the current study made an effort to establish the level of Christian involvement with diviners among the Akamba and the purpose for which they do so.

Diviners in the African community are believed to possess special abilities that enable them to act as mediators between the living and the spirit world. Given the various roles that they accomplish, they are revered as people who restore harmony especially where suspicion, anger and hatred may have brought division. In most cases, this harmony is enabled through rituals. A diviner acts as a moral guardian of the community (Kirwen, 2005: 189). Further study of an African diviner reveals that he is a source of consolation to those afflicted in body, mind and soul. Diviners are the mediums through whom societies and individuals are able to ward off evils that threaten human life, so that it remains lively and vigorous according to the wisdom of the ethnic group. They are the persons who walk with the living along the razor edge of life and give answers and consolation as one falls in and out of chaos. He/she accomplishes this role by is suing a verbal warning to those identified as culprits. Some diviners are able to foretell the future, something that in most cases unites those affected. For example, if a diviner foresees an impeding danger, the concerned persons come together to find ways and means of warding it off. Diviners play the role of tracking down the truth and of discovering the proper pattern of factors relevant to the client's problem. Kirwen compiled some seminar papers from various communities whose sources of data were both oral and written sources collected through reading, interviews and questionnaires. Since the above collections were not directly focused on the Akamba, this study pays a specific focus on the duties accomplished by the Akamba diviners. The researcher concentrated on observations and interviews for concrete, detailed and more precise data.

The Motive of the institution of Diviners in Africa

The institution of diviners is well established in Africa. Its continuity is an indication that it bears some benefits for both individual practitioners as well as society. The sole intention of this institution is the preservation of harmony in society and the integrity of creation. It is intended to promote life. Diviners are quite open about their practices today. In Kenya for example, it now common to read notices about the diviner hung on trees, walls and posts by road sides. From these notices, diviners from different ethnic communities and countries especially Tanzania claim to specialize on marital issues, enabling senior bachelors to find wives and vice versa, promoting business and making one prosperous in life. Since diviners see themselves as called to enhance harmony in society, any negative experience among the people calls for the need of a diviner to secure community balance once more. Some of these negative experiences are:

Recurring misfortunes- In Madagscar just as in many other African communities, repeated misfortune is an indication of a deeper underlying problem for which the diviner is consulted to establish its nature and cause. In this case, some form of placation may need to be carried out in accordance with the diviner's advice. In most cases, misfortune is attributed to ancestors' dissatisfaction with the behavior of their descendants especially for going against customary rules. Once the disorder is identified, offerings and sacrifices may be prescribed. At times charms may be provided depending on the diviner's assessment of the situation at hand (Peek, 1991:54).

Spirit possession- According to a study carried out by Barret (1989: 36) among the Turkana people of Kenya, spirits are believed to cause a wide range of afflictions. They are believed to cause both physical and emotional dilemma to human beings. It is also worthy noting that spirit possession is not only a threat to the individual but also to the whole family. Among Africans, spirits possess people with a purpose for which they cause trouble. Spirits of dead diviners can also possess a diviner to be. At times a certain spirit may want to communicate some message to some one. Attention to this is drawn through peculiar happenings such as one's animals speaking like humans, objects falling on the person, sickness and other forms of misfortunes as well as bad dreams. To cure this kind of affliction, spirit diviners are consulted for diagnosis and exorcism. Sacrifices and libations are offered to the possessing spirit in plea for release. Among the Turkana people of Kenya, the one for whom the sacrifice is offered identifies him/herself with the animal victim by touching it or by making a gesture before it is slaughtered. The killing of this animal symbolizes the death of the sick or possessed person. The person then requests to be reinstated properly into the order of the universe.

The above scholars writing on diviners do not suggest alternative ways of dealing with imbalance in society manifesting itself through sickness and suffering in human life as well as affliction by spirits. The researcher was curious to hear from the Catholic Christians how they dealt with the various problems affecting them especially spirit possession.

Witchcraft- Africans rely heavily on the advice and guidance of diviners in their efforts to cope with the problem of witchcraft. Diviners are believed to be spirit filled individuals endowed with extraordinary ability to comprehend "divine" things. People seek their assistance to discover solutions to problems that puzzle them (Parrinder, 1962:103). Parrinder adds that in some communities, diviners also play the role of witch-doctors whose primary task is to heal people who claim they have been bewitched. As Parrinder puts it, "it is against the evil activities of nocturnal witches that the witch-doctor operates in the public interest (Parrinder 1962: 106)". As witch-doctors, diviners seek the healing of those who are believed to have been injured by witches. Diviners are, therefore, chief agents in the curative campaign against witchcraft in Africa (Parrinder 1962: 107). The question of witchcraft is quite complex and yet common in society to date. Among the Akamba, cases of suspect witches being pulled by the neck to the diviner's hut for treatment are still common. In fact this is the reason for the administration of oaths (ndundu) that will be mentioned later in this chapter. During the field study, witchcraft came up as one among the many problems dealt with by the Akamba diviners in a bid to restore harmony and to reconcile witchcraft related conflicts.

For an increase of vital force- Making a general observation on diviners, Tempels (1969:45) informs that because of their ability to venture into the mystic world, the Bantu go to them to learn words of life, so that they can teach them the way of making life stronger. However, the question one would ask is whether some individuals could not visit the diviner to teach them the way of making life weaker for their enemies. Tempels omits the mention of this other side of the coin. In the study among the Akamba some respondents claimed that some people visited diviners in search of medicine for evil purposes. Whether this is true or false, it is beyond the scope of this study.

Miscellaneous reasons- Among the Africans and more specifically among the Yaka of Zaire, Peek (1991:113) observes that diviners are consulted in time of crisis such as, death, serious illness, deformity through birth or accident and repeated social failure. Their consultants want to establish both the cause and remedy to their problems.

In this section it has emerged clearly that negative experiences cause imbalance and disharmony in African cosmology for which many people seek the advice of diviners. Nevertheless, it is worthwhile asking ourselves how successful this institution is in as far as its intention of preserving harmony in society is concerned. For example, when the diviner points to a mother in law as the person responsible for the death of her grandson leading to family conflict, how much harmony has been achieved in such a situation?

From the above discussions it can be concluded that divination is considered valuable in times of crisis not only by Africans but also beyond the African frontiers. The next exposure will open us more clearly to the fact that belief in diviners is global.

Divination worldwide

In his study of mystical powers, Gehman (1989: 100-102) reports that divination is carried out to satisfy human curiosity about the future. He points out different methods of divination applied in different parts of the world namely:

)1 **Divination by examining dead animals**- Gehman refers to many diviners who examine the liver in order to divine the future. He says that this kind of divination was practiced by Babylonians in 2000 B.C. and today in Asia, Africa and in the West.

)2 **Divination by examining living animals (augury)** - This form of divination was used by the Etruscans of Italy, among the Melanesians and today by the priests of Borneo and the Philippines to foretell the future by interpreting the flight or action of birds.

)3 **Divination by examining the stars**- A type of divination practiced in Sumeria, Chaldea and Babylon, then later in Greece, Rome and Europe. This type of divination is used to predict one's fortune as well as his life, death, wealth, marriage, children and friendship.

)4 **Divination by mechanical means**- Gehman reports on the use of little tablets with written symbols by Romans. He also mentions that by 800 A.D they had already began using cards to predict the future. Ruth Montgomery one of those who used these cards says, "I simply have a person hold them, so that I can pick up his vibrations" (Unger, 1972:62). Gehman (1989: 101) further cites the use of pebbles to observe whether an odd number or an even number appears. This method is common to many cultures of the world including Africa.

)5 **Divination through dreams and visions**- Jeanne Dixon in the United States of America made use of this mechanism with her first

94

vision occurring in 1952 (Gehman, 1989:102).

)6 **Divination by possession**- This method has been used in Asia, Europe, America and Africa. German citing the example of a shaman in Siberia writes:

> The individual marked out by the might of the ancestors for shamanhood feels a sudden faintness and exhaustion…His limbs are wholly I ntensive; he snatches whatever he can lay his hands on, and swallows aimlessly everything he gets hold of –hot iron, knives, needles…afterwards casting up dry and uninjured what he has swallowed (Gehman, 1989: 107).

The above observations indicate that divination is not an African practice only but a practice universal to the human society. In studying divination, it is worthy noting that similar methods are employed both within and outside Africa. This fact points to the universality of this institution. The next big question is, if divination is universal "what does the Bible say about it?" A more important question to this study is, "if divination is universal, to what extent, have Christians been affected?"

Divination in the Bible

This dissertation would not be complete without consulting the Bible which is the voice of a Christian. Since the study is tackling the issue of the relevance of diviners to Christians, it is worth establishing the Biblical teaching on diviners. In this case, the study will consult both the New and Old the Testament.

The Old Testament

The practice of divination is not something new among the Israelites. The prophets in the Old Testament constantly warned the people against idolatry and the practice of false religions. 1 Samuel 28 records the case of Saul who went to consult a medium in view of receiving some crucial information from the spirit of Samuel. Since he knew Judaism did not allow this he disguised himself and went in the night (Vs 8). This act is an indication of a divided faith between the power of God and in the spirits. If Saul had full faith in God he would have implored His help for whatever revelation he needed. The same challenge goes to the Christians of the Catholic Diocese of Machakos. If those Christians who today consult diviners in time of crisis had full faith in the Living God, they would surely approach Him in prayer and unfaltering trust in His divine mercy for Jesus Himself says, "Come to me, all of you who are tired from carrying heavy loads, and I will give you rest" (Matthew 11:28). Another way of looking at it would be to accept the fact that, the one consulting has made a choice based on trust in the ability of the diviner to provide solution to the disturbing issue. This may therefore imply that in the diviner some people find consolation. It is the type of consolation received from diviners that this study seeks to understand.

According to Wilkermann (2004: 74-83) the greatest enemy of God is one who drives his people away from Him leading them to the belief in idols, to the practice of superstitions, mediums and witchcraft. The Mosaic Law forbids necromancy (Leviticus 19: 31; 20:6, Dt. 18: 11, Is. 29: 4). This same law declares that the search of truth from spirits of the dead is something abhorred by God. The Bible is very clear on what is unacceptable in the eyes of God namely; the practice of divination (Dt. 18: 10, 14, Daniel 2:27, 4: 7, 11, Isaiah

47: 13), magic, witchcraft and fortune telling (Leviticus 19: 26, 31, 20, 6, Exodus 22: 18, 2Kings 17:17). Isaiah (8: 19) says "But people will tell you to ask for messages from fortune tellers and mediums who chirp and muter" Ezekiel (22:28) endorses Isaiah's words when he retorts "they see false visions and make false predictions, they claim to speak the word of the Sovereign Lord but I the Lord have not spoken to them"

Peek (1991: 428) comments that the practices of diviners were different forms of oracle giving, through the manipulation of magical powers. Such practices were solely forbidden as they would incur God's punishment on the practitioner. Isaiah (3: 1-3) remarks that the judges, heroes, soldiers and their prophets, their fortune tellers and their statesmen, military and civilian leaders, their politicians and every one who uses magic to control events would have food and water withdrawn from them.

Rejection of any involvement with mystical powers in the Old Testament was aimed at focusing the hearts and minds of the Israelites fully on Yahweh. Any deviation from this would mean a divided faith something that God would not accept. This poses a challenge to the Catholics today who find themselves trapped in the milieu of seeking the help of diviners.

Since the present study was set to establish the relevance of diviners to contemporary Kamba community, information was sought on whether or not the Catholic Diocese of Machakos has put in place any measures of handling cases of Christians who consulted diviners. Details on this are to be found in chapter five.

The New Testament

The New Testament has no direct reference to the practice of divination. However, reference is made of Jesus and his follows engaged in the war against evil forces. Jesus cast out evil spirits from those who were possessed (Mark 1: 34, 39, 3: 11). In Jesus, the people come to learn of a new source of power contrary to their previous thought that such power came from Beelzebul the prince of demons. He teaches them that in order to counteract the power of evil, a different kind of power must be employed and in this case, the power of God. The same struggle with evil powers is mentioned of His followers. These warned the people against the worship of idols and witchcraft (Gal 5:20), murders and magic practices (Rev. 9:21, Rev. 18: 23, 21: 8, 22:15). They too cast out evil demons from the people (Mark 6: 7-13, Acts 5:12, 16, 8: 9-12, 19: 11-12).

Generally the Bible is quite unambiguous about magical practices. Reliance on any power other than the power of God is a clear manifestation of false religion. The Bible treats divination, auguries, dreamers and mediums as a class of people whose practices should be rejected by people, they are , not only distance themselves from God but provoke His anger against them.

In the history of the Akamba, cases of witchcraft have been common among the people. Although with lesser density today, the belief in witchcraft is still rampant. In fact almost all witchcraft cases are dealt with by the diviner. In the New Testament Jesus offers a new way of dealing with the forces of evil by calling upon His name (Mark 9: 38-39). St. Paul says "Build up your strength in union with the Lord by means of his mighty power" (Ephesians 6:10). Jesus presents the prayer of a Christian as the only thing that can overcome all evil

(Mark 9:29). He also indicates to the Christian community the importance of faith in God (Luke 17: 5-6). With one's life anchored in Christ there is no fear of witchcraft or any other form of evil.

The Catholic teaching on Divination

Catechism of the Catholic Church (1995) admits that revelation about the future is something often desired by humans. In this respect it states "God can reveal the future to His prophets or to other saints. Still, a sound Christian attitude consists in placing ones faith fully into the hands of providence and giving up all unhealthy curiosity about it" (No. 2115). This kind of revelation is in God's own time and choice. About divination, the Church states that all forms of divination are to be rejected; all that involves recourse to Satan or demons, conjuring up of the dead or other practices falsely supposed to unveil the future, consulting horoscopes, astrology, palm reading, interpreting of omens and lots, the phenomena of clairvoyance and recourse to mediums all conceal a desire for power over time, history, other human beings as well as the wish to conciliate hidden powers (No. 2116).

The Church also warns against wearing of charms or involvement with magical activities (No. 2117). By wearing charms, one risks placing trust in the charm other than in God who is the source of all power. In this study, the researcher was moved by the interest to find out whether Christians today and especially those of the Catholic Diocese of Machakos were involved in any of these practices and why. Although some information on this is found in the next sub-topic, a more detailed account on the Akamba and Catholic involvement with diviners has been placed in chapter five.

The Catholic encyclopedia (2003) makes it clear that actually the Church does not deny that, with a special permission of God, the souls of the departed may appear to the living and even manifest things unknown to them. However, necromancy is held by theologians as due to the agency of evil spirits. Because of its use of incantations, magical rites and demoniacal intervention, necromancy is viewed as special mode of divination and divination itself is a form of superstition.

The response of the Catholic Diocese of Machakos to the challenge of Diviners

Past experiences indicate moments of struggle between the Catholic Diocese of Machakos and ritualistic diviners. The latter moved across the community administering traditional oaths (Masya/Ngata/Ndundu) as witchcraft eradicators in 2000. In response, the Catholic bishop of Machakos Diocese then, the late Rt. Rev. Bishop Urbanus Kioko issued two pastoral letters in the same year, one to alert the Catholic population of the ongoing events and another to provide guidelines to the priests in dealing with those who had participated in the mentioned rituals. The following guidelines were stipulated in a pastoral letter of 29th August, 2000 addressed to all priests in the Diocese:

1) Those Christians who have accepted to take Masya/Ngata/Ndundu must be stopped from receiving Sacraments with immediate effect until further notice, and they should not receive any sacrament outside their own Parish.

2) Priests should not administer sacraments to these people until further instructions by Bishop

3) To be re-admitted to the sacraments, there should be a six months period of catechesis. This should be well planned by the priests.

The Catholic Church in Machakos is fully in harmony with the Biblical and the universal Churches' teaching on involvement with diviners and all those who use powers whose source is not clear. From the above guidelines to priests, it is clear that individual Christians are to nurture their own faith owing to individual consequences should they take part in traditional oaths officiated by diviners. However, this researcher does not think that stopping Christians who have participated in traditional oaths from receiving the sacraments is enough. In addition, it has been observed that this punishment is mostly administered with no prior instructions. Consequently, those affected remain in the same darkness that drove them to the ritual making them to fix their eyes on the punishment and not on the sin itself. Such people may not realize the seriousness of the offense. This calls for a review of this approach in order to promote a sound understanding and application of the gospel among the people. On the whole, believers are discouraged from involvement with diviners because their sources of power are ambiguous. Furthermore, some of the values upheld by diviners may not be concordant with the Gospel values and the Church's teaching. In the section that follow. The issues related to interaction between the gospel and culture will also be highlighted.

The Gospel and culture

The term gospel means good news of salvation of humanity channeled through the death and resurrection of Christ. St. Paul summarizes the content of the good news as justification by faith in Jesus Christ (Romans, 3:22). Jesus the saviour lives among his people as one who saves and brings new life to those ready to receive it. It is upon this dynamism that culture finds room in the gospel story. Culture is the sum total of all that make up life such as customs, traditions, rites, art, ceremonies, symbols, wisdom and institutions

(Walligo et al 1986:27). On the basis of this understanding, interaction between the gospel and culture becomes inevitable, especially in a growing and changing society.

In the case of Africans, the gospel entered Africa from the West by European missionaries. The gospel of Christ in its uniqueness presented to the African person a new dimension of life. Mugambi (1989: 1) uses the music analogy to explain what happens when the gospel enters into a new culture. Like a sweet melody it is transposed into a new key. When transposed from its biblical world to other cultural worlds, it undergoes change itself as well as causing these other worlds to change. It causes change in human institutions, creates new values as well as changing people's hearts. This is the effect implied by Isaiah when he says "My word is like the snow and rain that come down from the sky to water the earth. They make the crops grow and provide seed for planting and food to eat" (Isaiah: 55:10).

Most scholars among them Mugambi have write that, to most missionaries from Europe and North America, evangelization meant disorienting their objects of mission from "pagan, heathen, savage, primitive and barbaric" traditions (Mugambi, 1989:9). Missionaries in this case counted themselves the lucky custodians of the message of Christ while Africans could only count on their evil practices. This attitude was also observed by Kirwen (1987) in his study among the Tanzanians of North Mara district. He concludes that Missionaries were sent to Africa without any training in African cultures hence their hostile approach to African traditional values. Kirwen realized that despite this negative Christian attitude towards African cultural practices, the values and traditions of the African religions have continued to thrive through the ministry of diviners, religious elders and traditional priests. According to the researcher, this attitude entangled the smooth transmission of the gospel values to the Africans. Because of its background, many Africans saw Christianity as a foreign religion which promoted European culture while undermining their culture.

Adrian (1989:22) points out that, if the missionary message called for social change and the rejection of significant elements of the traditional order then the message could only be preached and implemented in the face of traditional authority either acquiescing or resisting. Resistance especially was not because Africans did not like the gospel message but because they had values that appealed to them more intimately. To turn away from values such as traditional healing would need replacement with a more convincing approach to human suffering. In addition, it is worthy noting that traditional practices among Africans have been passed on from one generation to the next. The breaking of this chain would therefore be resisted by many who hold firmly to its values.

Walligo et al (1986:22) indicate that when Christians fail to make Christianity part and parcel of them, the result is religious dualism. Gray and Luke (1978: 606-613) state:

A large number of African Christians find themselves divided into two personalities, one African and the other Christian. During the times of joy and peace they may be able to live as true Christians, but when crisis come, whether of illness, suffering, misfortune…they move back to their African personality and engage in ceremonies, rites and world view that have been constantly condemned by the Church..

Idowu (1973:205-206) concurs with the above observations in his assertion that African traditional religion is regarded as the final succor by most Africans. He gives the example of some practicing Christians who have traditional medicine smuggled to them in hospitals because, psychologically, it is more effective having been empowered by the traditional healer.

This dualism is an indication that Christ and his message have not yet been fully incarnated in the African world view. The birth of Christ into those aspects of life that revert Christians to their traditional ways is seen by the Church as the best approach to the problem of dualism. This birth is what we refer to as inculturation. Before making a comment on iculturation, it would be necessary to highlight on the levels of culture showing why a culture may resist the change intended by the gospel.

The levels of culture

Culture as a social phenomenon is the consequence of a people sharing a world view. For example, in the event of taking dowry to in-laws, it is a common practice among the Akamba for the concerned family to seek the company of relatives, neighbours and friends. In the African world view, individualism has no place in the community. The following levels of culture by Jacob and discussed by Shorter (1985: 35-37) are instrumental in the understanding of a people's behaviour as well as their response to the religious environment around them.

The industrial technical level- This is relatively a superficial level which is primarily concerned with technology, techniques of manufacture, communications and travel, sport and fashion. This level according to Shorter does not affect human beings permanently since it is in a constant state of flux. Nevertheless, given that its major concern is the material wellbeing of society, people could easily find themselves trapped in the world of endless concern with the superficial and trivial. Among the Akamba, having wealth in form of cows, goats, sheep, a productive farm and a healthy family among others is one's pride. It symbolizes God's blessings. In cases whereby instead of moving up the ladder things seem to move in contrary motion towards poverty, questions are bound to be raised. The experience of this researcher has been that some people want to find out from the diviner why things have fallen apart. Others will seek advice from the diviner on how to progress.

The domestic technical level- This is the level of family concerns. In its domestic nature, it deals with what is conventional and traditional such as traditional foods, manner of cooking, welfare of family members, leisure and the manner of performing various duties among other traditions. This is the level which affects the individual most. Among the Akamba, the search for the well-being of both parents and their children can lead to the treatment of a homestead as well as the individual family members by a diviner. During the study, it became quite clear that this form of treatment is also carried out in some Christian homes for the purpose of warding off witches and other evil people.

Level of values- The people of a particular culture, more often than not find themselves sharing particular preferred values. Although these values are a matter of priority and choice, they are passed on from generation to general through the process of enculturation. According to Shorter, this level is closely linked to the symbolical level which relates to the realm of ideas. He observes that it is this realm which governs the practical order and orients human behaviour. It is also at this level whereby meanings and values are expressed. Among the Akamba for example, family loyalty is a value, worship, respect, children and good health among other values. In the traditional setting, rituals play a key role in the preservation of life and harmony in the community. This is why for instance, traditional worshipers walk round a given area with a ritual goat annually in plea for God's protection and blessing for the community. This study was anchored in the researcher's quest to realize the values attached to diviners by Christians. One of the key values discovered was healing. Every one in this world from time to time may experience health challenges of one kind or the other. The search for healing is therefore a common phenomenon owing to varied health encounters. One time a Christian student remarked to this researcher that, if only he would find some one to treat his eyes, he would not care whether the person is a traditional healer or a modern medical practitioner.

Level of a world view- This level defines the manner in which people of a particular culture understand and act towards the world around them. It comprises the experience of the spiritual world, the physical environment and of other human beings. For the Akamba, the universe is imbued with immense power which can be tapped at will by different people for different purposes. It is believed that particular people such as diviners, medicine men and women as well as witches have access to this power more than any one else. Owing to this belief, in time of crisis, the Akamba consult diviners because they are believed to act as a link between the spiritual and the material world. In

106

addition, the Akamba hold the human person responsible for the maintenance of cosmological balance without which life in the universe is at stake.

Religious understanding of reality is at the heart of culture. Shorter (1985: 137) observes that it forms the inner parts of culture. At this inner most level of the cultural personality one encounters more resistance to change than at any other level. In his opinion, it is easier to change the outer practical levels such as fashion and leisure than values or a people's world view. The researcher is in full accord with Shorter's view because what people believe in, is the decisive factor in understanding their core reality. Consequently, any attempt to divert them from that which they hold dear is bound to meet with resistance unless an alternative is put in place. Such a replacement must concur with the people's needs and expectations or else it will proof a futile effort.

Among the Akamba for instance, there is still a looming belief in witchcraft. Beneath this belief is the view that only a diviner can disarm a witch or reverse the effects of witchcraft in a victim. This explains why some Christians have been found to consult with diviners in search of healing and charms to ward off witches among other reasons. Involvement with traditional oaths such as *ngata* has especially posed a real challenge to evangelization in the Diocese. This is due to the fact that evangelization propagates values that are at times foreign to those that dominate the culture. In this case, evangelization constitutes a fundamental challenge to culture hence the role and meaning of inculturation.

Conclusion

Based on the literature so far consulted, we realize on the one hand that, the institution of divination presents itself as a universal institution. Citing the case of Africans, diviners are viewed with vitality because they have a key role to play in the life of the community. Some of the roles they accomplish are; diagnosing and healing diseases and ailments, carrying out rituals and counseling, serving as prophets, priests and custodians of esoteric knowledge. It is therefore because people see in diviners a charisma that enables them to capture and at the same time to reveal hidden knowledge that they consult them.

On the other hand, the Bible discourages all divination practices. Despite its reality, the practice of divination is viewed as a manifestation of false religion hence unacceptable. The literature reviewed revealed that although Christians are aware that the Church does not welcome the practice of divination, they still go for it in time of difficulties. Perhaps the African belief in spirits contributes highly to this contrast. The literature reviewed revealed that African divination relies heavily on revelations from ancestral spirits and spirits of other members of the community. As a practice it applies different procedures ranging from simple to more complicated ones as already discussed in this chapter. The practice of divination continues to permeate African cultures despite the widespread Christian faith that relies on the power of the Holy Spirit. This chapter therefore points to a possible conflict in the life of a Christian who pays allegiance to traditional practices involving diviners while at the same time confessing faith in God through Jesus Christ.

CHAPTER FOUR: RESEARCH DESIGN AND METHODOLOGY

Introduction

This chapter presents the research design and methodology used to generate data in answer to the study problem. It consists of six main sections. Section one expounds on the research design used in the study while section two discusses the population targeted for information. Section three describes the sample and sampling techniques. The fourth section highlights on the research instruments used in the collection of field data and section five exposes the procedures followed in sourcing information from the respondents. The final section of this chapter elaborates on the procedures applied in the presentation and analysis of data.

Research design

This study was mainly qualitative. Unlike quantitative research, a qualitative study opens the possibility for understanding latent, and underlying issues allows for thick descriptions, flexibility in the data collection procedures and lays emphasis on people's lived experience hence allowing the researcher to identify the meanings that people place on events, processes and structure of their lives.

The perspective of the study was phenomenology, rooted in the discipline of philosophy. The phenomenological approach in the study of religion was first employed by Edmund Husserl a German philosopher (1859-1938). Patton explains Husserl's idea of phenomenology as the study of how people describe things and experience them through their senses. According to him, understanding starts with perception of the senses followed by description, explication and interpretation (Patton, 1990:40-41). Phenomenological approach describes the meanings of a lived experience. This approach was found appropriate for this study because, interaction between the community under study and diviners is a lived experience that needs keen investigation in order to establish its sources and mode of operation.

In line with the direction of this study, the naturalistic design was most preferred. This type of a design directs the researcher to observe and understand phenomena as they occur in their natural settings.

Naturalistic design was preferred for this study because it enabled the researcher to observe key events such as, a divination session hence paving way to the understanding of cases, tools and methods used by diviners to provide solutions to their clients. Naturalistic inquiry paradigm involves a systematic collection, analysis, and interpretation of data in order to provide descriptions and accounts of social events and objects of research in their natural setting. By applying this paradigm, the researcher was able to penetrate into the natural settings of participants, their stories and experiences with diviners while at the same time maintaining 'epoche'. This interaction facilitated the disclosure of the role played by the diviner among the people.

Target population

The informants of this study were diviners, traditional elders and traditional worshipers, Government leaders, Church leaders and ordinary Christians. Diviners, traditional worshipers and traditional elders are viewed by this researcher as custodians of traditional religion, and its beliefs as well as practices. Their choice was therefore driven by the researcher's desire to

110

acquire solid cultural information from them. People that had interacted with diviners among them traditional worshipers were also believed to possess first hand information about these traditional specialists and their practices. Their experiences greatly enriched this study. The choice of Church leaders including priests was based on the fact that they are more often than not actively involved with Church affairs and are therefore more informed about the undertakings of the Christians than the rest. The researcher assumed that some of them and especially priests had the experience of listening to different cases. During interviews with Church leaders it emerged that their close interaction with their members had equipped them with vital information related to the problem under study. Since these were the same people often consulted by Christians in time of dilemma, they had adequate information to share in relation to Christian involvement with diviners. Ordinary Christians also participated in this study. As mentioned earlier on, long before engaging in this study, the researcher was already aware of some Christians who consulted diviners in time of crisis. By this study therefore, the researcher intended to establish the extent to which Christians actually visited diviners and why.

Sample and sampling techniques

This thesis is not a full scale census meant to meet every single member of the targeted population. Rather, it is a micro-project designed to address the question of the relevance of diviners in Machakos Diocese. Further still, being qualitative by nature, the study had as its central aim, to provide in-depth information on the activities of diviners and why these activities appealed to the contemporary Kamba community. In order to acquire the quality information desired by the study, a total of 60 people were expected to participate as respondents in the field research. Although this figure may seem large for a qualitative study, it was justifiable on the grounds of the researcher's desire to gather information from a variety of clusters in the Kamba community. Samples were drawn from three parishes; Ikalaasa (Machakos County), Thatha (Machakos County) and Kasikeu (Makueni County). The three parishes are more than 100 km apart. From each parish, 20 respondents were to be interviewed by both the researcher and her research assistants. The 20 respondents from each parish included adherents of traditional religion and government leaders.

For selection of respondents, the study applied non-probability sample designs. Both purposive and snowball sampling techniques were used. To select sample units from among diviners and traditional elders, both purposive and snowball sampling techniques were applied. From these categories, the first respondent was selected purposively after which the snowball technique was applied to identify the next 5 diviners and 5 traditional elders. From each parish, 2 diviners and 2 traditional elders were reached for information. To select sample units from among traditional worshippers, priests, Christians and Church leaders, purposive sampling was utilized. These are more open or rather known groups in the community and were therefore easy to identify and to access. From these clusters, 12 traditional worshippers, 3 Government leaders, 9 Church leaders and 24 Christians were selected. Purposive sampling was preferred in the study because it enabled the researcher to select sample units that were felt to have a higher possibility of providing the desired information. In the selection of sample units from various categories, the question of gender was considered irrelevant since the researcher's interest was concrete information regardless of who volunteered it. The table below demonstrates a summary of the total number of respondents for the entire study.

Table 1: Distribution of respondents by parish

Respondents	Ikalaasa Parish	Kasikeu Parish	Thatha Parish
Diviners	2	2	2
Traditional Elders	2	2	2
Traditional Worshippers	4	4	4
Government leaders	1	1	1
Church Leaders	3	3	3
Ordinary Christians	8	8	8
Total	**20**	**20**	**20**

Description of research instruments

In order to obtain the information desired for the study, the following instruments were used:

In-depth interview guide

Five types of interview guides were designed: for diviners, for traditional worshipers and traditional elders, for Government leaders, Church leaders and ordinary Christians. All interview guides consisted of open ended questions aimed at soliciting information from sixty respondents.

a) **In-depth interview guide for diviners**- The diviners' interview guide sought information from six diviners on their area of specialization, nature of issues dealt with, methods used in divination and nature of their clients. The researcher was quite interested in hearing from the diviners themselves of the role they perceived to play in the community, why and how they interacted with Christian clients.

b) **In-depth interview guide for traditional elders and traditional worshipers** - This instrument sought to provide information on the elders' experience of the diviner as one of the traditional religious specialists, the kind of needs they presented to him/her, their attitude towards the diviner and what they thought about the future ministry of this specialist, particularly for Christians. From this category eighteen respondents were reached for information.

c) **In-depth interview guide for Government leaders-** This guide aimed at collecting information on the Government experience with diviners and its stand on their practices. Three respondents were interviewed.

d) **In-depth interview guide for Church leaders-** This instrument was designed to gather information on the leaders' understanding of diviners, their role in society, Christian involvement with diviners and why, and the Church's view on this practice. In total nine respondents were interviewed.

e) **In-depth interview guide for Christians-** This instrument was intended to gather data on the peoples' understanding of a diviner, his/her perceived role in the community, on the question of Christian involvement with diviners and why, and whether it affected their Christian faith or not. Twenty four participants were selected for interviews.

Observation guide

This instrument contained guidelines on how and what to observe about diviners and their clients especially during divination sessions. This guide which comprised a list of items to be observed targeted at least one diviner. It was designed laying keen interest on the methods used by the particular diviner. What the diviner did and said was keenly observed in order to enable the researcher to assess the reality of the particular method used in responding to a particular problem. For example, a diviner may try to convince a client that it is through pebbles that a solution had been reached while in actual sense it was by interrogating him/her that a solution was achieved. This assessment benefited the problem under study because it provided a basis for the judgment whether it was the methods the diviners used that attracted clients to them or something else.

The researcher was also interested in observing the behavior of a client during a divination session for example, the body language. Justification for the use of this tool was the researcher's view that interviews alone do not provide rich nor concrete data. Combination of both interviews and observations was therefore instrumental in the collection of necessary information key to the study.

Description of data collection procedures
Field data collection whose main target was the selected sample was chiefly acquired through interview and observation schedules.

In-depth interview schedules
Two different types of interviews were conducted:
  a) **Face to face interviews**- Face to face interviews were conducted to gather first hand data from diviners, traditional elders and Church

leaders. The researcher met each of these respondents on one to one basis by the help of an interview guide comprising open ended questions. Separate days were scheduled for each of these clusters for smooth flow of information. The researcher both directly and through the research assistants made appointments with each interviewee. This was to facilitate the psychological preparedness of the respondents. In the course of interviews, both the researcher and the assistant made notes. From time to time, the researcher repeated key responses to the interviewee for affirmation. This skill was employed to ensure that a true record of the interviewee's ideas had been done. Photos were taken at times but only when the respondents permitted it. Although a tape recorder was in plan for use, this skill did not materialize. The recorder at hand was a visible one. An attempt was made on two occasions but the diviners questioned why it was necessary to record their voices. One of them said "I will speak louder". On realizing that the recorder was not a familiar tool to those for whom it was intended, the researcher decided to discard it to avoid causing discomfort which would otherwise interfere with their freedom to volunteer information.

b) **Focus group discussions**- This was applied on traditional worshipers and Christian respondents. To solicit information from these clusters two groups of each were formed. Research assistants who had been prepared ahead of time assisted in moderating some of the group discussions. This took place at the Parish compound and at homes. Interview guidelines containing open ended questions were availed to each research assistant. Two research assistants assisted in each group. One of them assumed a secretarial role while the second one together with the researcher ran the interviews. Responses were preserved by recording on notebooks.

Observation schedules

In order to observe the on-going activities, the study employed the direct observation skill. The researcher observed a divination session by diviners. This technique allowed for collection of detailed and comprehensive information from the people without necessarily taking part in their activities. This gave an opportunity to the researcher and her assistants to take notes. Where the observer was not in a position to document observations on the spot, this was accomplished later as soon as opportunity was secured.

Validity and Reliability of instruments

The following skills were applied to ensure that the instruments used in this study were relevant to the research quest, and that the information gathered by their use could be objective and reliable.

Triangulation

As already demonstrated in point 4.4 and 4.5 of this chapter, a variety of data collection methods were applied namely; in-depth interviews, focused group discussions and observations. These strategies enabled the researcher to assess how the different methods agreed with the content (data from the respondents). As can be deduced from the previous discussions on methods, the different types of interviews as well as observations were more or less designed to solicit comprehensive and more less similar information from different types of respondents. This was in order to detect any contradictions as well as to note similar trends in thought and experience. Interviews for example, confirmed what had been observed.

Detailed description

This is yet another way of checking validity and reliability of research instruments as well as of data collection. By use of the methods selected for this study, the researcher tried as much as possible to provide details of events, people interviewed and observed. Information acquired in relation to the topic on diviners and their relevance to the contemporary Kamba community was reflected upon though indirectly in the previous chapters and is presented in detail in the next two chapters.

Member check

Interview records were repeated to individual interviewees from time to time during the session. The researcher did this with the intention of receiving confirmation from them as to whether what had been recorded was their true contribution or not. In fact one woman and a traditional worshiper (K. Kitulya, personal communication, March 17, 2008) dictated to the researcher what to write and of which was later read to her for confirmation. Written notes were also read to those respondents who wished to counter check their responses. By so doing, respondents actually approved of what had been recorded.

Audit check

Finally, this researcher ensured validity and reliability of instruments used and collected data by keeping all records related to the research being done. Keeping track of events, discussions and field observations facilitated verification and confidentiality, especially during analysis of data and discussion of findings.

Data analysis procedures

Analysis of data was part and parcel of the research process. As soon as the first piece of data was obtained, the researcher immediately began with the analysis process. Three main procedures were taken into account namely:

Data reduction

At this level of the study, establishment of files and coding field notes was a vital exercise. Field data was organized into meaningful categories and themes, which were then summarized in view of the study problem, in order to provide the required responses to the stated questions. This process of selecting, condensing, focusing, and transforming the field data was for the purpose of manageability as well as making it intelligible in favour of the issues under study. The process of data reduction also enabled the researcher to decide which aspects of the assembled data needed to be emphasized during the actual description and which ones needed to be minimized.

Data display

At this stage, the already organized data was displayed in word. Data falling under the same categories was narrated and described in details. An integrated approach was adopted whereby both field data and data from written sources provide the content for discussions.

Drawing conclusion and verification

After the presentation of data, the researcher then interpreted and assessed its meaning and implications for the questions being addressed by the study. Conclusions were then drawn from the emerging data as will be seen in chapter six. As the researcher drew conclusions, a review of the data was constantly done to maintain a link between them. This exercise finally led to the articulation of several recommendations necessary as a step towards the promotion of faith in the Catholic Diocese of Machakos and indeed the entire African community.

CHAPTER FIVE: A PRAGMATIC VIEW OF THE AKAMBA DIVINER VIS-À-VIS EVANGELIZATION

Introduction

This chapter presents and discusses findings from the field. The content presented here is the fruit of personal interaction with, and reflection on information acquired from different respondents: diviners, traditional elders and worshipers, Government leaders, Church leaders and ordinary Christians. This experience was made possible through the help of several field assistants. Interviews were conducted on each of these groups. The observation skill was applied mainly on diviners and their clients. For the entire study, sixty people were anticipated for participation but only fifty eight successfully participated. Those who missed out were one Christian and an area chief. Efforts to have these two participate in the study were thwarted by unforeseen circumstances. Nevertheless, those who participated provided the information sought for by the researcher in line with the stipulated research questions.

The six research questions outlined in chapter one of this dissertation formed the basis for the physical organization of this chapter. Responses related to each question were coded, organized and presented under the same theme.

This chapter has been organized into the following themes: The Akamba concept of diviners, issues addressed by diviners in contemporary Kamba community and their favorite methods, reasons for Christian attraction to diviners, impact of Christian involvement with diviners in the Catholic Diocese of Machakos on other members of the Christian community and methods of evangelization applied in the Diocese in relation to Christian involvement with diviners.

The Akamba concept of diviners

To begin with, the researcher set out to capture views from different respondents on their concept of a diviner. The underlying purpose for this question was to enable the researcher to enter into the people's field of understanding of a diviner. The whole question was triggered by the researcher's belief that behind every attraction or hatred directed to a person is a mass of knowledge and experience of the object of attraction. Responses to this question were gathered from traditional leaders and worshipers, Government leaders, Church leaders and ordinary Christians. Diviners were exempted from this question since the researcher's concern was other peoples view about them in order to assess whether their views of diviners are a contributing factor to their attraction towards them or not.

Traditional elders and worshipers

These strata comprised all traditional elders and traditional worshipers in the sample frame. Although separate sittings were scheduled for these two groups, their responses were compiled into one piece due to their commonality. By holding discussions with them, the researcher noted that these people shared a common view of diviners. They all described diviners as traditional specialists, healers, counselors, friends of the community, comforters, revealers of enemies of the community such as thieves and witches, reconciler's in time of conflict, revealers of hidden knowledge and prophets. Their responses were in harmony with Mbiti's view of African diviners as revealers of the mysteries of life (Mbiti, 1995:177). This harmony is an indication that the diviner is someone that is widely known and accepted as a special person in the African society.

A number of these respondents likened diviners to Syokimau, one among the oldest known prophets among the Akamba. He is believed to have lived long before the coming of Europeans to Africa. He is remembered for his prophesy about the railway line and the train as a means of transport cutting across Kenya. According to them, there is no one in the community who can adequately replace diviners since they played a role unique to them. Musau Makali a shrine attendant remarked, "These people have been there since the beginning, they are part and parcel of the Akamba culture and they are there to stay" (M. Makali, personal communication, March 12, 2008). Muthini Kalamav (personal communication, March 9, 2008), a traditional worshiper added, "Theirs is a special call from God for the welfare of the community and not for themselves" 9th March, 2008). Other respondents such as Mweleva (N. Mweleva, personal communication, March 7, 2008) laid more emphasis on the esoteric character of the Akamba diviner. They both expressed with such conviction that diviners possessed a special ability to communicate with the spirits something that enabled them to break through mysteries in human life. They were in consensus that diviners made life an easy path to tread by providing answers to complex issues in society.

The understanding of diviners by traditional elders and worshipers tallied with the view of diviners in other parts of Africa as indicated in the literature review. For example, Olupona (2000:87) mentions that diviners restore and reconcile estranged relationships for a harmonious and habitable universe. Like the Akamba elders and traditional worshipers, Turner (1969: 42) and Akiiki (1982: 73) view diviners as people who possess special powers because of their association with the spirit world.

Apart from the common view of diviners as beneficiaries of the community, some shrine elders, Nyamai Mwonga, Kituma Mulwa and Kitulya Kikuvi (March 16-17, personal communication, 2008) pointed out that although there were many genuine diviners practicing for the benefit of the community, some of them were conmen/women and could not be relied upon. These sentiments were echoed by Mwangu a former shrine attendant but now a convert to Christianity (M. Mwangu, personal communication, March 14, 2008). A genuine diviner according to these elders is known by the fruits of his/her medicine and revealed message. This revelation is a point of strength to those involved in the work of evangelization. The sentiments shared by the traditional elders harmonize with the teachings of the Bible that reject all forms of lies and falsity (Exodus 20: 16).

Encounter with traditional elders and worshipers revealed that diviners still existed and that they were still held with high esteem by some members in the Kamba community. During the interviews this researcher observed that, traditional worshipers including their elders honored their culture and held it with great value. They were convinced of what they shared and spoke with seriousness, understood too well the demands of their culture and their role to preserve it. However, during the interviews, majority of them expressed the fact that a culture holds depths that must be handled with great care or else one will become victim of its demands. This could be felt from the seriousness with which they expressed it. It was at this point that this researcher was able to begin realizing the connection between their view of cultural practices and beliefs and their concept of diviners. Because culture and its components presented to human life complex situations that at times were difficult to cope with, the diviner was necessary to provide a break through by demystifying these situations.

Government leaders

As already noted, two Government leaders were successfully interviewed instead of three as earlier planned. The two appointments made with the third respondent were unsuccessful. Instead he sent apologies. Those interviewed were chief Joseph Ngui and Sebastian Mang'ee. The two chiefs acknowledged the presence of diviners in their areas of jurisdiction. Both were in harmony that diviners were traditional specialists that per-occupied themselves with cultural issues such as broken taboos (uvitanu), mysterious happenings such as thieves getting stuck on the stolen items, healing mysterious and incurable diseases and ending witchcraft crises in families and clans. (M. Ngui, personal communication, March 16, 2008) firmly expressed his belief that diviners were experts in diagnosing and also healing diseases that modern hospitals fail to deal with such as, those resulting from broken taboos. The strong point posed by these two chiefs in their concept of diviners is that diviners possessed knowledge that is not common to all. One of them remarked that even without going to school, diviners were able to penetrate situations in human life that people with degrees could not understand. He gave the example of someone who had lost some luggage on his way home. Since he was familiar with the people he had traveled with he went to them one after the other and no one owned up. Finally he brought in a diviner and called on elders to witness the search for the thief. The diviner made use of those present to accomplish his job. He held a round shiny stone and mentioned one name after the other while holding the stone near the eye of the person he had chosen. At the mention of one particular man, the stone disappeared into the eye for some time. The person mentioned admitted the crime.

Chief Mang'ee (J. Mang'ee, personal communicatin, March 30, 2008) appreciated diviners as traditional doctors, as people who could tell their clients about future dangers and enemies and, who might have bewitched them. He also added that diviners have powers to neutralize the powers of a witch as well as providing protective medicine against witchcraft. Both Mang'ee and Ngui indicated that they had personal experiences of some deeds by diviners that promoted their belief that these people worked with supernatural powers.

Church leaders

Among those asked to comment on what they knew of diviners were priests, catechists and leaders of Church Stations. Both the catechists and the rest of the lay leaders shared that diviners were cultural experts. According to them, people viewed diviners as experts in deaeling with cultural and non cultural related issues such as broken taboos, witchcraft cases and search for wealth. They also pointed out that people visited them for healing. Their views were closely linked to those of the traditional elders and worshippers, and Government leaders in that they all thought of diviners as people with a special role to play in so far as some cultural issues were concerned.

The four priests, who aired their views on this question, based their views on their experience with their Christians. R. Mutisya, 15th March, 2008, C. Musyoki 19th, March, 2008, C. Kilonzo, 29th, March, 2008 and N. Munyweiya (personal communication, March 29, 2008) admitted their awareness of

Christian involvement with diviners. They also expressed knowledge of the presence of diviners in various parts of their parishes. According to them, traditionally people viewed diviners as healers, magical workers, prophets especially when misfortune befell the community and as spiritual guides. Consequently, some Christians privately consulted diviners in time of crisis.

Ordinary Catholic Christians

Although group interviews were conducted on ordinary Christian respondents, there were cases when the researcher held discussions with one or two of them due to poor observation of time as scheduled and poor communication by the organizers. They presented diviners as healers, as specialists who provide protection to people from witches, as people who communicate with the world of spirits, people who deal with culture related problems such as taboos.

Observation of Christians during the interviews revealed fear in some of them. When asked to express their understanding of diviners some of them immediately said "I have no personal experience of a diviner but I will share from what I have seen happen to others or heard about them" From this statement the researcher came to realize that some of the Christians would not share openly forcing the change of approach from group to individuals whenever this was appropriate. For those Christians who eventually revealed their involvement with diviners, it was not immediate but gradual. During interviews with different respondents including the Christians it was revealed that Christians visited diviners in secret. From this background we can deduce that although some Christians may have had personal experiences with diviners or their families, revealing this to another Christian may not be easy. All in all, the different Christian respondents reached out for information expressed their knowledge of the diviner whether out of a personal experience or from secondary sources. This is an indication that the diviner is not a stranger to the Akamba community and more so to the Christians who stand at the core of this study.

Having established the Akamba view of diviners in contemporary times, we shall move on to discuss at a deeper level the particular issues addressed by these diviners. This is aimed at establishing the link between Christian attraction to diviners and the problems diviners deal with among the people.

The diviner's identity in the community
The question addressed here is the diviner's identity, area of specialization and methods applied. As can be observed from the table, two types of diviners were identified. These were ritual diviners and diagnostic diviners. Against each type, the particular issues dealt with and methods applied have been highlighted.

Table 2: Distribution of diviners according to issues addressed and methods/tools used

Type of diviner	Issues addressed	Methods/Tools used
Diagnostic diviner (mundu mue wa kititi)	Physical illness -Curses -Recurring misfortunes -Witchcraft -Marital problems -Love issues -Economic prosperity -Employment -Prophesy -Spirit possession -Prophesies	•Divination (kwausya): **Common tools:** -a bow, half a calabash, a gourd, musical instruments such as, an accordion (mbeve) and a pitch pipe (nzumali) •Healing rituals •Medicinal herbs
Ritual diviner (mundu mue wa ng'ondu)	-Physical illness -Curses -Oaths -Recurring misfortunes -Broken taboos -Harmful medicines	-Cleansing (Kuusya) by use of *ngo'ndu*

Figure 2: Examples of tools used by diviners

Photos by research assistant, March 2008

The above figure displays some tools used by diviners. On the top left hand side is an accordion being played by the researcher. Every Akamba diviner desires to have this musical instrument. According to them, they play the accordion to conjure, to sooth and to entertain the concerned spirit working in collaboration with the diviner so as to come round and accomplish the divination process through the diviner. However, Ndulu disclosed to the researcher that any other person playing it would receive no response from the spirits. On the right hand side is Mutio and her husband with whom she works in time of herbal treatment. Divination gourds, oil for massage, a mirror, some special clothing, a whisk, sea shells, a horn and baskets for storage of divination tools are at the bottom. According to some respondents, the mirror is an instrument used to sermon culprits in social life or those intended for harmful purposes such as death.

Types of Diviners

Diviners among the Akamba fall under two broad categories; according to their areas of specialization and methods used as presented on table 5.3.1. Both types of diviners serve different needs in the community and complement each other in their roles. Since they belong to different areas of specialization, at times the same client may be handled by a diagnostic diviner for discernment and by a ritual diviner for cleansing. Syokwia (personal communication, March 8, 2008), some diviners interplay in the two areas as in her case, while others may perform in one area only depending on the nature of one's call as revealed with time and sealed at the time of inauguration (kukunulwa uwe). The following are the different types of diviners:

Diagnostic/gourd diviners (*Awe ma kititi*)

The second category of diviners is distinguished from purely ritual diviners by the use of a gourd hence their name. This type of divination is by inheritance. The gourd of a Kamba diviner contains pebbles (mbuu) that one is born with some pebbles while the rest are collected from a special tree known as *kivuu*. According to Kasuki, a Christian respondent and one of those born holding small round seeds, this rare incident is believed to symbolize the future call of this child as a diviner. N. Kaleli (personal communication, March 8, 2008) convincingly shared that the one who commissioned her brought to her some pebbles in a dream. Her gourd therefore contains pebbles she was born with and later vomited, those given to her in a dream and those she collected from the designated plant. Diviners believe that the pebbles one is born with are symbolic and not real. They are tiny seeds appearing in the naval. According to Ndulu she vomited them as a grown up girl confirming her call as a diviner. Since most of the diviners belong to this group the following summary will be helpful in understanding their role in the community.

Table 3: Some examples of diagnostic or gourd diviners

Diviner	Areas of specialization
Syokwia Mutua	-Diagnosis divination -Prophet -Economic progress -Healing with herbs -Witchcraft
Ndulu Kithuka Mutio Musau	-Diagnosis divination -Prophesy -Midwifery -Rituals (perform rituals on women only)
Ndulu Kaleli	-Diagnosis divination -Witchcraft -Healing through massage -Rituals
Vata Ngaa	-Prophesy -Divination

Figure 3: Diagnostic diviner and prophet

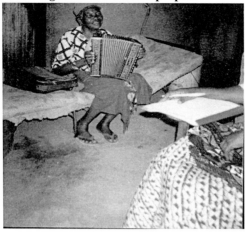

Photo by the research assistant, March, 2008

Syokwia Mutua (blind) demonstrates to the researcher and her assistant how she uses the accordion. It was amazing how she sweetly played it and sung from the background. She admitted that this tool is used for the purpose of conjuring spirits during a divination session.

All the six diviners we interacted with welcomed us warmly even without an appointment. In the company of different research assistants, the diviners wanted to know the intention of our visit. Experience with Syokwia (personal communication, March 8, 2008) was the most striking. For the last nine years she had been blind but ever growing stronger in her divination. One of her sons assisted with the collection of herbs from the forest. When the researcher and her assistant entered the diviner's house, the first question to was, "why do you want to know about divination and you are not diviners?" To this bold question we expressed our need to be conversant with the traditions of our people and even to write them in books for preservation. "Okay" she said, "and here I am".

Syokwia willingly responded to all the questions directed to her. She narrated to us how as a young girl she diagnosed people's problems through clairvoyance under the supervision of her two grandparents before the gourd would be entrusted to her after marriage. The two grandparents sat at the door post and acted as mediators between her and the clients. This was a form of training to this young girl although she did not understand their motive at the time.

When asked how she would know what response to give to a client she attributed this to an inner voice that she referred to as the voice of an angel that revealed things to her. After about 30 minutes of interrogation, the diviner turned to me and said,

Diviner- It has been revealed to me that you are in a special vocation; you are leading many people but that you are living on the other side

Interviewer- which side?

Diviner- The other side away from us, and you have not done what the Akamba culture demands

Interviewer- What do you mean by that?

Diviner- You have not gone back home to offer what is needed for you to be with us. As of now, you are on the other side of the river and not with us

Interviewer- Realizing that the diviner was beginning to manifest the researcher tried to divert her from it. It was then at this point that the researcher asked her if she could allow us to see some of her tools. Her first

135

reaction was that the owners may not be happy with her and that they might beat her up when we are gone. However, we insisted until she gave in to our request and produced the following tools:

The divination bow - She uses it to conjure the spirits with whom she works. This is done by tickling the bow with a small stick. Bursts of song mixed with intervention of conversations characterize the use of this instrument.

The divination gourd – Containing pebbles that she uses to determine the cause of a problem. According to her, the guiding spirit is involved in determining the number of pebbles to be released and their meaning. This diviner attributes everything to the intervention of the spirits.

The Accordion - The diviner plays this instrument during sessions to appease the spirits, to implore their cooperation and to entertain them. She also mentioned that as she plays the accordion there is some secret conversation between her and the spirit at work. She explained that the love of music by the spirits is one reason why in each diviner's home *kilumi* drums are to be found and from time to time a dance is performed in their houses. In this house, the researcher noted some two long drums hanging on the wall. The diviner was open to declare that there were other things which she would not show us out of obedience to the directives issued to her by the spirits with whom she works. This means that diviners have some secrets they keep to themselves and that there is an owner of the work. This raises questions about all that goes on in divination. It seemed to the researcher that in as much as a lot is revealed to those who are not diviners, still much more remained hidden. Since clients did not actually enter into discussion with the attending diviner about their work, a lot of details were missed out. This researcher thinks that although this institution presented some ambiguity, clients were more interested in having their problems solved than understanding the detailed operations of diviners.

This diviner referred to her guiding spirit as "an angel" from God the Creator. What was not clear to her was whether she worked with one or more angels because only one appeared to her at a time but that this angel was a familiar figure. Although she did not come out clean on this issue, the researcher learned from other diviners that they worked in association with ancestral spirits.

Syokwia's stand painted a picture in the researcher's mind that the use of the term angel was in order to give an impression to Christian clients that whoever guided her in divination was just like the rest of the Biblical angels of God. In connection to this she at one point said "As a solution to their problems, I ask my clients to offer an animal sacrifice just as Abraham was asked by God to do, when God's angel directed him to the sacrificial lamb" Since Syokwia had gone through the Catholic catechesis as a young girl, the Bible was familiar to her. She even claimed that at times she quoted the Bible to her clients. According to the researcher, reference to the Bible in a divination session may lead some clients to mistake it for a Christian practice which is not the case. Although she no longer practiced the Christian faith, it seems to this researcher that Syokwia had no problem integrating relevant Christian teachings to her traditional faith. She said that she loved Christians and was disposed to help them in their needs. Her positive attitude towards her clients is a point of strength in her ministry.

Other areas of specialization for Syokwia were healing the sick through rituals and herbs, the jobless, those seeking for marriage partners or are disturbed by their spouses. She also foretold the future and explained by use of clairvoyance current and on-going issues. Those who think they have been bewitched consult her too. According to her, such victims must undergo the ritual of unbinding (kuvinguwa) them from the bonds of witchcraft or spells cast on them. To those who feared that someone may bewitch them, they visited her too for protective medicines. Such clients undergo a contrary ritual in which, charms to dispel the powers of a witch (kuvingwa) are applied on various parts of the body. This ritual involves making incisions on various parts of the body of a client such as, in the chest and at the back of the neck. According to these diviners, the medicines put in the incisions act as a curse to any attempting witch and will result to death unless the bewitched person is willing to spit on the dying witch to reverse the situation. Hellen Katuku (personal communication, March 15, 2008) and E. Muthoka (personal communication, March 6, 2008) confirmed having gone through this ritual when they were young through the decision of their parents. Ndulu Kaleli performs a similar ritual.

Ndulu Kithuka, Syokwia, Ndulu Kaleli, Mutio and Vata are all consulted about rain among other issues. This particular role is strictly between them and shrine elders who arrange for a dance (kilumi) in the diviner's home during which they believe the spirits are best disposed to point out how far or how close the rains are, what type of sacrifice is to be made and in which shrine. The diviner can also call for the meeting in case she happens to have a particular message to convey to the elders commonly known as *andu ma nthi* (people of the world).

Figure 4: A diagnostic diviner and midwife

Ndulu Kithuka displaying her working tools; Photo by the researcher, March, 2008. Ndulu Kithuka uses the accordion, the gourd and the bow. On the wall of her house hung three long drums which she said had a role to play in her divination endevours.

Ndulu Kithuka above who was in her mid 60s specialized in gourd divination (uwe wa kititi). She said that at birth, two pebbles were found in her hand as a sign that she was destined to become a diviner. This vocation was inherited from her grandmother (her father's mother). She at the same time inherited all her tools namely; the divination gourd (kititi), the divination bow (uta), an accordion (mbeve) and a small basket (kathango). In divination, all the above mentioned diviners seek to establish the cause of a problem, its nature and solution. All the diviner respondents were in agreement that in divination, there is either a direct or indirect communication between the diviner and the spirit of the one from whom the call is inherited.

Midwifery, although not strictly attached to divination is practiced a lot by most female diviners. However, M. Mutio (personal communication, March 16, 2008) clarified that midwifery was revealed to her as one of her designated roles as a diviner. Apart from the particular roles specified on her list, she asserted that, her gift was all round and that she attended to clients with different problems without any hitch.

Observation and interaction with different diviners during the field study enabled the researcher to realize that there were strict procedures in divination. However, although most of them were common to all, a few differences were also realized. Before divination kicks off, the diviner dresses officially as dictated by her/his spirits. This is followed by spreading of the divination skin (from a Leopard or Deer) (Lindblom 1969: 126) on the floor and arrangement of other necessary tools. In case a leopard hide is not attainable, a goat skin can be used. Some diviners ask the client to sit on the divination hide while majority of diviners provide a stool or a chair. This is followed by submission of divination money. Although the use of money is not cultural, this mode of payment is as old among the Akamba as the introduction of the coin during the colonial period in the country. For some diviners, money is given before the exercise as a sign of one's commitment while for others it is submitted at the end of the session. M. Kasuki (personal communication, March 8, 2008) informed this writer that the diviner does not touch money before or after the session. All the money is placed on the animal skin. This means that a gift of money has been given to an animal and not to the diviner. This skill is employed to safeguard the diviner from the client's curse should things not work well.

R. Muunda (personal communication, March 26, 2008) also shared with the researcher that some diviners entered into blood pact with clients before the divination process commences. This is done by making cuts on their hands and licking one another's blood as an assurance to the client that what is going to happen is free of malice and fraud. Licking of each other's blood is a covenant in its real sense. At the same time it exposes the parties concerned to the risk of contracting HIV/AIDS virus. Another respondent, M .Kasuki (personal communication, March 28, 2008) added that in some cases, the client is asked either to sit or sleep on the animal hide after which the incision is done. Blood from both the diviner and the client is then mixed with honey and poured on the top and bottom of their feet to indicate the sealing of the covenant. This covenant impresses upon the client the seriousness of the event just about to take place. The whole process is beneficial to the diviner in that, whatever the client is asked to bring he/she will have to bring it in fear of breaking the covenant. According to Kasuki, this ritual is performed for the safety of the diviner should things not go well with the client. The belief is that the client cannot curse or raise a case against the diviner after this ritual. This study views these preconditions in the divination ministry as detrimental to the health of a client in that they may inflict more fear than peace in her/him. Entering into a blood covenant is an act of commitment to the entire process and an assurance that the client will not hold the diviner responsible should anything go contrary to their expectations. Such a cultist act is discordant with the Catholic faith and teaching. As noted elsewhere in this dissertation, it is only the blood of Christ received at the Eucharistic celebration that is binding to the Catholic faith.

In the second step of divination, the diviner seeks to know the history of the problem and the persons involved. Should the client be unwilling to share their part of story with the diviner he/she will say "*nuundulila yau*" (you are putting a block to the divination process). The sharing about the problem is done in form of a discourse between the two. The researcher's understanding of this is that, solutions to the problems of clients are shaped by the background shared. That is why the diviner will not accept to proceed unless the client comes out clearly on what they know about their own problem.

The third step is the divination itself during which all instruments are used interchangeably. After rattling the gourd, the diviner discusses results with the client. This is repeated after the bow. The divination gourd is never emptied out completely during the process. This is an indication of continuity otherwise complete empting of the gourd would mean termination of the process. The number of pebbles thrashed out each time conveys a particular message. For example, according to M. Ndulili (personal communication, August 20, 2006) and N. Kaleli (personal communication, March 8, 2008);

- Two pebbles reflect the footsteps of an evil man (Nzamba) or a woman (Syongua) walking towards the home of the client. Usually these are footsteps of a witch or a wizard,

- Three pebbles indicate that the cause of the problem is to be found within the family

- Four pebbles indicate clearly that a man is walking towards the homestead

- Five pebbles specify a woman as the one causing trouble to the one suffering

- Six pebbles indicate that the ancestral spirit in charge of the family is the one causing trouble

- Seven pebbles signify that the cause of the problem is a woman's. It also follows that the woman is a witch hence the term "muonza u mwai" or the deadly seven and has therefore bewitched the person in question.

On the contrary, according to Ndulu Kithuka and Syokwia, the number of pebbles released from the gourd speaks uniquely about the situation at hand. According to them, there is no common interpretation regarding the number of pebbles released during a divination session. For Syokwia (personal communication, March 8, 2008), the meaning of each number of pebbles thrashed out is dictated to her by the spirit at work with her. This means that different diviners have their unique experiences during divination, though there is much in common.

For example, M. Muthoka (personal communication, August 24, 2008) a traditional worshiper, consulted a diviner in search of advice regarding her daughter who, for many years could not find a husband. For her case, in the first cast two pebbles came out while in the second five were released. The interpretation was that an evil woman was the cause of her misfortune. Maswili believed in the diviner who eventually carried out witchcraft unbinding rituals on her Christian daughter. Although this girl married soon after that, it would be difficult to determine what it was that barred her from doing it earlier than this.

Generally speaking, by listening to and observing diviners, made one marvel at how much they can accomplish even without formal training. By their very strong inner conviction, diviners influenced the faith of their clients drawing them to believe in their words and medicine. A closer examination of the diviner's ministry revealed that the words mentioned to a client such as, "a

143

witch is after you" or "a taboo has been broken" bore a lot of weight and meaning to the extent that the instruments were used simply to strengthen and to confirm the word. The instruments as well as the singing and ambiguous noises mesmerized the waiting clients and enhanced their trust that their needs were being attended to.

Examination of the issues dealt with by diviners revealed that diviners among the Akamba deal with different problems affecting human life. For instance, they provided solutions to relational problems, illness and economic challenges. This discovery was quite significant to the problem under study. Shorter (1985: 3) observes that in today's approach to healing "there is no wholeness. It is for this reason that the tradition of integral healing practiced in the Black cultures of the Third World have so much to teach us" The researcher concurs with Shorter that the human person craves for integral health. If the Church slides a little in this effort, it should not be a wonder to find some of her members walking away in search of integral health. The Akamba diviners present themselves to the people as broad spectrum healers. This explains to some extent why some Christians today are attracted to them.

Ritual diviners (Awe ma ng'ondu)

This type of diviners specializes in cleansing rituals (kuusya). Ng'ondu is a special cleansing solution prepared from special plants known as Waithu, Mulinditi and Ndata Kivumbu. Seeds of these plants are dried, pounded and mixed with water. The mixer is then sprinkled on the complainants by use of a particular cleansing plant called mutaa which produces a pleasant scent. Seven pieces of sticks of another plant known as Mukengesya are then placed in the mouth of the victim one at a time and he/she is commanded to vomit all he/she

144

has swallowed. Each stick is then pulled out of mouth and thrown away in faith that the person is now cleansed. After this the victim is asked to move to another spot as a sign that he/she has been restored to normalcy.

An interview with different diviners revealed that ritual diviners were useful in cases of broken taboos. Illnesses resulting from this complex issue are generally referred to as *uvitanu or thavu*. Other issues dealt with are curses (kiumo) and oaths (muma). J. Makula (personal communication, March 29, 2008), a very famous ritual diviner from Kasikeu, uses *ng'ondu* in his cleansing rituals. Among his clients in the month of March 2008, was a couple that had broken a sexual taboo. This researcher learned from Makula that, the Akamba customs forbade a couple from bathing or coming together as husband and wife after participating in the funeral rites of a close relative until seven days are over. By human frailty this couple was unable to stay away from each other for seven days. When this happened, it scared them forcing them to visit Makula for cleansing. In his own words, this was a Catholic Christian couple, aged 25 and 35.

Although this researcher may not understand much of this traditional ritual, it may not be remote to compare it to the Catholic reconciliation rite in terms of its motive. What the two rituals do is to wipe away guilt that one has suffered as a result of the evil act. However, the traditional ritual has also an additional value of soliciting money from clients. To Christians, it inflicts into them a second guilt conscience. Justifying the traditional type of cleansing M. Mutio (personal communication, March 16, 2008) ruled that acting contrary to cultural demands is a defection from one's culture hence punishable by the ancestors who continued to ensure the preservation of the human culture.

Another taboo mentioned by N. Kithuka (personal communication, March 26, 2008) was in connection with death. According to her, if a woman dies and another is married and stays in the same house before cleansing is done, it is taboo. Traditionally, it is believed that the second woman will also die unless cleansing is carried out. A good example is Kituli, a traditional worshiper who today lives in a single roomed house after abandoning a three roomed house. After the death of his two wives, he had to move out of his house in order to marry a third one whom he now lives with. The diviner had to cleanse the house and its surroundings, as well as planting medicines at strategic corners of the compound to ward off witches.

Another serious taboo is the belief that if a woman delivers and the child dies, and another woman visits or touches her, and happens to conceive before she is cleansed, her child will also die. Lindblom (1969: 101-105) points to the same belief. In December 2007 a lady narrated to the researcher how she had delivered alone and, due to lack of proper management the baby died after an hour. When this happened, all those in the compound including her sister in law disappeared in fear of contamination, something she could not grasp. Her brother buried the body by himself. Although members of this family are Christians, they still held firmly to their traditional beliefs and practices. To these Christians there was more fear of breaking with their traditional faith than acting against Christian charity. In view of this behavior, it goes without saying that, if they had acted in breach of the particular taboo, approaching a diviner for cleansing would have been the obvious step.

Traditional believers and elders interviewed on the question of the issues dealt with by diviners confirmed that ritual diviners were experts in cleansing people from evil effects of life. M. Mutuvi (personal communication, March 14, 2008) indicated that acting contrary to the taboos of the Akamba, curses and oaths can cause serious problems to the life of a person such as physical illness, mental disorders and misfortunes. A ritual diviner whom this writer planned to meet turned down the appointment the last minute because a lorry driver had taken him to his home. This driver had recurring accidents and had twice knocked and killed two pedestrians. To call a diviner for a cleaning ceremony was a sure indication that he knew his problem and its solution as well. The step taken by the driver may serve as an affirmation that when people have been socialized in a particular thought or belief, everything else is likely to be judged according to the dictates of the same social setting. That is why a Christian who has been brought up in such an environment will find it normal to consult a diviner regardless of his/her faith. This shows that in the diviner there are some benefits that people seek in order to experience harmony in life.

The above experiences point to the fact that some of the issues dealt with by diviners are spiritual by nature. For example, in the case of broken taboos, victims seemed to suffer guilty conscience which they believed could only be eliminated through a traditional ritual. This means that ritual diviners are still useful to those who believe in traditional cleansing rituals hence their relevance to the Akamba.

Figure 5: An example of a ritual diviner

Photo by research assistant, March 2008

Makula on the left, from Kasikeu in the company of his wife charts with the researcher. In his hands is some of the stuff he uses to heal people. He has such deep faith in his herbs to the extent that he despises Western medicine at all cost. Although he claimed to be baptized (Joseph), he neither identified himself with the Christian concept of healing nor with Jesus the healer.

Why Christians are attracted to diviners

In the previous discussion, we realized that the Akamba diviners engage in various activities by which they alleviate suffering and pain among the people, and which impede their experience of abundant life, either as individuals or as a community. As such, many people of whom Christians are part, visit diviners for example in time of illness and misfortune with the aim of being restored to the wholeness of life. In the following discussion we shall spell out

148

the different reasons for which Christians especially consult diviners.

Although this question sought to understand the reasons underlying Christian involvement with diviners, it was addressed to all units in the sample frame. This is due to the simple fact that, the same Christians visiting diviners interact with traditionalists at the home, as clan members and as people of the same village. If this be the case then, the observations of other members of the community is a necessary flavor to what the Christians would say about themselves.

During the interviews all respondents admitted to this writer that diviners were in existent among the Akamba and that both Christians and non-Christians visited them for various reasons. K. Ndula (personal communication, March 17, 2008) remarked that, the question of Akamba interaction with diviners is a tradition that lies deep in them and a very hard to die culture. Mutune Kituli (personal communication, March 7, 2008) a former Catholic and now a traditional elder, and who was once married to a diviner said to this writer, "To tell you the truth, diviners are used to having interrupted nights because nights are the best hours for those who fear exposure and especially Christians" This is an indication that diviners are still valued by some of the Christians. Some of the sources of Christian attraction to diviners are:

Diviner as a cultural specialist
Among the Akamba, diviners are viewed as the strongest existing specialists in various issues related to the cultural practices of the people. Traditional elders and worshipers were particularly loud on this point. They contended that, the Akamba regardless of their religion, from time to time found

149

themselves faced with questions and problems that were beyond the family, clan or village elders' wisdom. In this case, it is the diviner who has maintained a firm institution on the preservation of culture that can provide a better answer to such cases. According to them, the diviner stands out as a symbol of a culture that is alive and active.

Family background/environment

Other respondents cited one's background and environment as closely linked to Christian involvement with diviners. Among them R. Malinda and R. Kilavi (personal communication, March 28, 2008) said that some Christians went to diviners as a family practice. These Christians had observed that, these families had the diviner at the center of their day to day life to the extent that a diviner was consulted in time of family dispute, during moments of crisis or engagement in new activities such as joining a school or embarking on a long journey. In this case, involvement with diviners for such people was in the normal flow of the family stream. Rose, a retired officer, had observed that, those people who were brought up seeing diviners in and out of their homes, with none of their parents expressing concern about it, fixed it in their minds that it was something "normal" and She said, "Later in life during life challenges, the highest possibility will be for one to apply the same technique as applied by his/her parents to arrive at a solution". She cited the example of her own father whose parents believed in diviners, something that sunk deep in him to the point that later in life they became his consultants and doctors. She had witnessed at least two diviners who had come to treat her father against snake bites. Although her father saw a lot of snakes, she said, he was never bitten. The Akamba have a saying that a finger that once scooped the remains of porridge from the pot never forgets it (kala kaasuna kayulawa).

Those Christians brought up to believe that the diviner is the answer to their questions in life continues to cherish him/her despite the new faith that is foreign to their customary faith.

Belief in the diviner as a mystic

A group of elders (personal communication, March 16, 2008) pointed to diviners as key people in the community. According to them, indigenous Akamba diviners posses an ability and the skill to penetrate into the mystical world, diagnose diseases and provide solutions to dilemma's of human life. Kimilu (1962:88) is in harmony with these elders that diviners share in the powers of the divinities particularly the ancestral spirits. J. Maweu (personal communication, March 28, 2008) one of the Church leaders, in accord with the above views remarked, "Belief in the existence of spirits and especially the ancestral spirits promotes the common belief among the Akamba that, diviners have a link with spirits and therefore understand better the spirit world". He gave the example of some people hearing voices of unseen and unknown beings at night. According to him, such an incident may coincide with other family problems which the victims may relate to the voices heard leading them to consult a diviner to interpret for them the mystery. These respondents expressed that both traditionalists and Christians today visited diviners in search of hidden knowledge which they believed could be accessed through the diviner. J. Mang'ee (personal communication, March 30, 2008) remarked:

> Diviners are trusted by the Akamba as depositories of mystical powers to the extent that even pastors visit them at night. People cannot do without them because it is true that diviners have very strong powers.

According to Mang'ee, magical power that is portrayed by diviners is more attractive to the people than what priests or pastors exhibit. What seems to be communicated here is that people want to have prompt solutions to their problems from diviners rather than being called upon to pray, believe and wait for God's will to be done.

Dispenser of mystical powers

According to both Christians and traditional worshipers, diviners share with clients the powers to manipulate situations in their favor. Some of the mystical power shared is for common good for example, the power to heal certain diseases or to reverse negative situations. N. Ngunga (personal communication, March 27, 2008) gave the example of Ndulili a former traditional healer of snake bites but now deceased, who acquired his healing powers from a certain diviner. The researcher had the opportunity of interviewing him on his healing practices. According to him, he had to pay a bull for the initiation rites. Skills on how to prompt the healing power into medicinal herbs were passed on to him.

Other respondents shared that those needing witchcraft powers can also obtain them from diviners. Among these were J. Kasuki (personal communication, March 29, 2008) who viewed diviners as rich sources of evil power. This view was echoed by J. Makula (personal communication, March 29, 2008) a ritual diviner and M. Ngumbi (personal communication, March 16, 2008) a traditional worshipper. According to these respondents diviners have the power to disable a witch's power and to unbind those already affected by it by performing certain rituals. According to these respondents, some diviners are witches themselves.

The contention by these respondents that, some Akamba today visited diviners in search of mystical power point to the belief and conviction that, this power actually does exist in diviners. While this researcher does not disregard the fact that mystical power exists in people, she however opposes its misuse for example, in the case of witchcraft. Negative utility of any skill or power instills fear in people and can lead to paranoia.

One respondent pointed out that some people among them Christians had no apologies to make for using objects invested with mystical powers for example, to attract more customers to their business or even to stir up chaos in a rally if the proceedings were not in their favour. J Makali (personal communication, March 12, 2008) narrated his experience as an attendant in a hotel. The ownership of this hotel was shared between two people who were not quite friendly to each other. One afternoon as he waited on customers one of the share- holders came in and dropped some object under one of the tables. Within seconds clients began fighting each other breaking any utensil they could lay their hands on. Whatever was dropped under the table was believed to have been invested with evil powers that sparked off the commotion among clients. This incident marked the end of this hotel business.

The Akamba experience is an indicator of the complexity of the spiritual world around us. It also points to the inability of the human mind to comprehend fully the non-empirical world. Belief in the diviner is an attempt to understand the operations of the world beyond senses. From time to time, People want to experience and even to have a share of these mystical powers.

The diviners' charm muthea (kamuti)

The Akamba diviners claim to manufacture a certain herbal medicine *muthea* which according to them opens opportunities for job seekers, those who want to progress materially, those searching for a lover/threatened love or people threatened by a particular situation or person. C. Katulu and A. Ndolo (personal communication, March 17, 2008) confidently shared that this was happening to people of all faiths. According to them, the present job insecurity in the country where by many Government workers had been retrenched was caused fear leading some people to diviners to acquire some charms for protection. These respondents justified the use of charm asserting that life had become a hard nut to crack hence the need for reinforcement. Love portion was also mentioned by some traditional worshipers as well as Christians. J. Makula (personal communication, March 2008) a ritual diviner remarked that, diviners did not only serve with love portion those who wanted a particular man or woman but also used it themselves to capture women clients. According to him, this explained why male diviners had more than one wife. Respondents claimed that there was no uniformed manner of administering charms. The charm may be in the form of powder that is put in the food of an intended victim. It can also be hidden in finger nails and released secretly at will. In of search of riches, some people obtain different types of objects from diviners under strict instructions. Some of these objects are worn on wrists, neck, around the the waist or as instructed while others may be stored in the house.

Security

Some traditional elders expressed their conviction that genuine diviners were a source of security to society. M. Kivoti and K. Mbuu (personal communication, March 27, 2008) in support of their chief claimed that today some diviners provided their clients with charmed rings for economic prosperity. According to these respondents, these articles plus the diviner's verbal assurance were a great source of security to those in possession of them.

On the same breath, some Christian interviewees argued that those who sought treatment against witchcraft suffered a lot of insecurity. Witchcraft related rituals acted as an assurance that one was fully protected. Some of the interviewees testified to their knowledge of treated families but declined to mention their names. Although this researcher later received details of these families, confidentiality must be observed. According to these respondents, the diviner accomplished his protective role in the family by planting medicines around the homestead. This researcher is a witness to this. Some time in 2007, a Christian family revealed that some things had been planted by a diviner in their compound through the arrangement of one family member, and that most of them were no longer comfortable with these items. Although the family wanted these items removed some of them would not move close to the site and would not even talk as the pots were dug out. Deep in them there was fear of the consequences, an indication that belief in the power of these medicines still possessed them.

A keen observation of these respondents revealed that some of them had significant knowledge on how the diviner provided security by a practical use of herbal charms and rituals while others had no experience. This means that although the experience of fear of the evil power of witchcraft existed among the Akamba, still this would not be generalized.

The search of solutions to the witchcraft menace

The study further revealed that Christians were attracted to diviners due to the broad problem of witchcraft. Belief in witchcraft is still looming among the Akamba though with less weight as compared to the pre-Christian era. According to J. Kasuki a Christian leader (personal communication, March 29, 2008), the name *Muoi* (a witch) stems from the word *Mue* (a diviner). According to this respondent, the powers of a witch are linked to the diviner who is in turn linked to the spirits. A diviner according to him has full control over witches in that they possess the skill and the charm either to revitalize or to neutralize a witch's power. Apart from Makula, all the five diviners interviewed during this study described themselves as experts in dealing with witchcraft issues. Giving a personal testimony to this, Chief J. Mang'ee (personal communication, March 30, 2008) acknowledged having the experience of people accused of practicing witchcraft and who, when action was taken against them, they either died or ran mad.

The view that witches had a link with diviners was attested to by all the respondents. They were all categorical that those Christians who believed they were bewitched went to diviners for healing while others went for protective medicines against witches. This too is in harmony with what the researcher found out in a study carried out on witchcraft and its effects on Christian faith in Muthetheni Parish (1999). During this study, the researcher learned that Christians went to diviners either to be healed from witchcraft related problems or for protective medicines against the same. She also noted that, the problem of witchcraft was not localized to the Akamba community but that it was a universal phenomenon just as divination is.

Witchcraft eradication rituals (ngata/ndundu)

All Christian respondents pointed out that traditional oath ceremonies were a real threat to faith. A group of Christians interviewed from Ikalaasa (personal communication, March 17, 2008) expressed their disappointment about some traditional practices operating in several places whereby, if someone in a family or clan was suspected of practicing witchcraft the solution was to force all the married members into a witchcraft eradication ritual. A case narrated to the researcher (Parish name withheld), was that of a priest who once stepped in to save his Christians from being forced into the ritual. The traditional elders organizing the ceremony held him captive for some hours threatening to administer the oath to him too. This experience according to them instilled guilt and covered with shame the affected Christians. They were ashamed of being associated with witchcraft. They also suffered guilt for causing the arrest of their Parish priest by the elders. These respondents concurred with Kasomo (2003) in his study among the Christians of Mwala Machakos and with Munuve (2001) in his study that covered the whole of the Catholic Diocese of Machakos. These studies confirmed the use of traditional rituals to solve witchcraft and curses issues. From the above experiences, one sees a deep rooted desire among the Akamba to maintain harmony in the community leading some Christians to bow to family or clan pressure to participate in traditional rituals. Nevertheless, despite the disappointing aspect of being forced into these rituals especially on the part of Christians, the researcher learned from some respondents that the ritual restored peace and harmony in

157

the family and in the clan. It reconciled people that were once enemies and feared each other due to witchcraft accusations. These respondents are in agreement with Olupona (2000:87) who describes an African diviner as one who reconciles restrained relationships in the community. Submission to this external pressure is what Kalilombe describes as taking into account community solidarity to avoid attraction of suspicion of being witches. According to him, the widespread fear of witchcraft and sorcery practices to counter it, are signs of the central importance of kinship solidarity.

The oath rituals are practiced as a means of eliminating evil in the form of witchcraft from the community. Perhaps it is time to state that, the diviner has all through the history of the Akamba been at the center of witchcraft cases and so to remove him from this center, a more aggressive replacement has to be put in place.

Belief in the diviner as a healer
This study found out that some Christians resulted to consultation with diviners due to the inevitable experience of human suffering. The researcher learned from both Christian and traditional worshipers and diviners that due to the challenge of many and complicated diseases among the people, diviners were looked upon as healers in the community. The kinds of healing are spiritual, physical and psychological. At times some people claim to be tormented by evil spirits that must be cast out. The family of Mutua and Kavuu who claimed their daughter was afflicted by an evil spirit visited several diviners in search of deliverance but according J. Mutanu (personal communication, March 13, 2008), no help was obtained. Despite Kavuu being a Catholic, she did not believe that such a case could be managed in the

Church until Mutanu brought it to the Parish Priest through whom the girl was finally set free.

Integral healing is the desire of humanity and people engage differently in its search. The Church document, Gaudium et spes (No. 3, 1966) states, "For the human person deserves to be preserved; human society deserves to be renewed" All respondents cited the diviners' healing power as a key value sought by clients. N. Munyweiya (personal communication, March 29, 2008) one of the respondents gave his personal experience of a man he found in Makula's home (ritual diviner) lying on the floor with his whole body swollen and could not walk. He had been ill for close to a year. Makula attended to him for three consecutive days washing him with the solution of *ng'ondu*. A week later Fr. Nicholas, met the man walking on his own and in perfect health. Another incident of healing was narrated by J. Maweu (personal communication, March 28, 2008) whose brother had been taken ill for quite some time. As a young boy he accompanied his father to the diviner's home to consult him about his brother. The diviner diagnosed witchcraft as the cause of his brother's problems. For some days his sick brother had to live with the diviner during which several healing therapies were administered until he was well. Among other treatments, the sacrifice of a goat was made and blood poured as libation to the spirits and a small piece of its skin fixed on the wrist of his right hand. This same practice was noted by Peek (1991:54) among the people of Madagascar. On the whole, diviners are widely accepted as healers in society. What remain questionable are the elaborate rituals at times used by diviners in their healing sessions and their nature as well. One of the common prescriptions was offering of a sacrifice by family members on behalf of the sick person. The purpose of this sacrifice is to appease the offended spirits or spirit. This researcher was made to understand that spirits enjoyed drinking blood, hence the need for constant sacrifice of a goat in order to win their favour in time of need.

As far as physical healing is concerned, the Diocese has one hospital, Bishop Kioko hospital which is moderately equipped. Almost in every Parish there is a dispensary. However, these medical centers handle only a limited number of cases due to distances, finances and limited number of facilities. Some people have to travel long distances to access these medical centers. Still, modern clinics are limited to the treatment of cases that are organic by nature. Therefore, finding answers to culturally oriented issues remains one of the current challenges to pastoral workers in the Diocese. For example, as a young girl, the researcher recalls seeing a certain woman crying out like a baby. This continued for a whole day and she was unable to stop it. Finally, a diviner was taken to her house. The diviner asked for some beer which he offered as libation mentioning different names. This was followed by a unique form of handshake between the diviner and the woman. Both crossed hands in the form of a cross. This form of greeting is referred to as *kunengwa mukono* literally translated as "being given a hand". During the study it was revealed that, through this greeting, it was not the crying woman but the disturbing ancestral spirit in her who was being beseech ed to relent. After the greeting she calmed down. Cases of this nature cannot be diagnosed through clinical tests and therefore remain a big challenge to the Church in the Diocese.

Doctor of broken taboos

Another group of interviewees pointed out that the Akamba culture was still active and that to this today there were still many people holding on to their traditional beliefs and practices. These views were echoed by J. Makula (personal communication, March 28, 2008) a specialist in cleansing rituals who described diviners as people who understood deeply the traditions and customs of the community and who in turn acted to preserve them. According to him, there are certain cultural issues that can only be handled by a diviner. Among the issues mentioned were broken taboos linked to different rites of passage such as birth and death rituals. M. Kituli (personal communication March 7, 2008), a former Catholic and now a traditional worshiper identified the respect of taboos as a major draw back to Christian faith. In line with the traditional practices, he ascertained that broken taboos will always culminate in a crisis situation forcing the victim to seek remedy in the traditional ritual of *ng'ondu*.

In support of the diviner as a specialist of traditional beliefs and practices that dip people into problems, a Christian respondent who declined to be named revealed to the researcher that she and her sister were taken to a diviner because they had used their father's blanket in his absence. Their mother convinced them that if they failed to be treated they would neither have a stable marriage nor children.

Relevance of the diviner to Akamba community is seen in the persistent belief in some families that diviners have the power to either revert or prevent suffering in human life. It is therefore the observation of the researcher that diviners continued to receive respect from the people as key dealers in moral and spiritual issues that infringe on the traditions of the people. This challenges Christians to heighten their belief in the reality of God's power working in His Church, through His own chosen people such as priests.

The search for practical and immediate answers to problems

Diviners are believed to be practical and prompt in providing answers to problems in human life. Chief J. Ngui (personal communication, March 16, 2008), a practicing Christian observed that practical solutions to people's problems were more enticing than telling them to pray and wait indefinitely for God's time. His experience was that diviners were not only practical but also prompt in providing answers to problems. His case in point was that of a village that lodged to him a complaint of their stolen cows. He used all possible means to find out who the thieves were but to no avail after which the complainants sought permission to search for the thieves by themselves. After a while, suspects were netted down and brought to him in the company of a large number of villagers and a diviner. The chief was made to sit and watch without intervening. The diviner then began to pump air into a pipe. As air filled the pipe, abdomens of the thieves began swelling. Within no time there was a lot of noise from the thieves as their stomachs protruded to a bursting point. The diviner then called them together and without any resistance they owned up and were made to pay double the number of cows stolen. On submitting to the offense, the diviner followed the same procedure but this time, not pumping but releasing air out of the pipe after which the swollen abdomens were back to normal.

The researcher admits that practical and immediate solutions to life challenges are very convincing and that they can lead masses diviners in search of remedy. When Jesus multiplied the bread and fed the five thousand men they said "Surely this is the prophet" (John 6: 14). The next day when Jesus crossed over to the other side of the lake they followed him and he said to them "I am telling you the truth: you are looking for me because you ate the bread" (John

6:26). The crowd following Jesus discovered in him a man that was prompt in answering to their biological needs. Because of their ready answers to daily problems therefore, diviners attract many to themselves. A certain Christian respondent (name withheld) remarked that the Church was no longer practical in meeting the needs of her members. She reiterated that there were more promises and indifference to people's suffering than there were answers hence, the experience of lapses to diviners.

Availability and approach to clients

Worth noting is the view extolled by some Christian respondents (personal communication, March 8, 2008) that some of them suffered a feeling of emptiness in their Christian faith since there was not much follow up by the priests and their catechists after baptism. According to them once baptized, the only consistent on-going faith formation was the Sunday homily which was not sufficient. Concurring with this, some respondents added that, some Parishes had only two priests or one who could not sufficiently attend to the needs of every Christian since there was only one office day in a week for the entire Parish population. According to them this paved way for the weak Christians to turn to diviners for consolation when faced with challenges of life. According to them diviners were always available and ready to attend to those in need.

M. Kianga a traditional worshiper (personal communication, March 7, 2008), described a diviner as a person who acts with a lot of patience, listens attentively and takes great interest in a client. Some Christian respondents (personal communication, March 6, 2008) regretted that some of their Pastors had no time to listen to their long life stories hence leaving them dissatisfied even after a consultation. According to them, some people were enticed by the keen attention and empathy accorded to them by diviners.

During interviews with diviners, the researcher observed that diviners were welcoming people, warm hearted, patient, concerned, use of convincing language and confident about their supernatural abilities. This approach not only promoted the client's confidence in the diviner but also created a therapeutic atmosphere. A suffering soul needs a counter experience to generate fresh energy for survival. Christians just like any other members of the human society desire to be understood, listened, given empathy and made to feel part of their immediate community. Lack of these according to some Christian respondents, created a porous faith situation leading some of them to retrogress to their traditional specialists.

Methods of divination

The study established from the diviners as well as other respondents that each of them was different from the other. All the diviners interviewed by the researcher confirmed that during divination sessions, different methods and dressing styles were adapted. This was in accordance with the directives of the one from whom the powers were inherited. The study also established that diviners used different tools such as accordions, gourds containing pebbles and a divination bow. This concurs with the findings of Mbiti (1992: 178) in his study of other African countries. Among the Yoruba, pebbles are made use of alongside other tools. When the diviner makes use of these objects, the answer to the client's problem is discerned and interpreted in line with the material outcome of the pebbles. In the case whereby a certain diviner is used as a medium by particular ancestral spirits, communication is done through dreams and visions. At this point, what the researcher judged magnetic to clients were the skills applied, the art and the complicated procedures that breded the desired cures to the disturbing issues.

Interviews with some Christians who once followed this way revealed that, the methods used were also intended to convince the clients that the entire process was not just controlled by the diviner but rather by some supernatural powers. The methods used by diviners contributed highly to the conviction of clients that these specialists were well equipped and that they possessed the ability to access information that is inaccessible to ordinary people. As already discussed, it is important to note that the methods used by diviners are practical and provide an immediate answer to the problem at hand. Within a short time the diviner is able to turn what seemed mysterious into ordinary. Whether the solution presented is true or false, this is not the concern of clients so long as a solution is presented to them at the end of the divination session. Observation by the researcher revealed that, the methods used by diviners coupled with their complicated outfits impacted strongly on the psychology of their clients who saw them as mystics.

Affordable charges

Diviners in the Akamba traditional community are cheaper as compared to hospitals. This opinion was aired by both Christians and traditional worshipers. On the question of payments, all the six diviners were categorical that their charges were never fixed but relative. Ndulu Kaleli and Mutio Mutua (8th and 16th March 2008), mentioned that although their charges ranged between 500 and 3000, everything depended on the nature of treatment. At times, the charges could be lower than five hundred shillings depending on the diviner's assessment of a client. According to Syokwia (personal communication, March 8, 2008), her angel whom she also described as *mwiitu mulaika* (Angelic lady) was responsible for defining the amount of money to be paid by each client. Diviners accepted both money and goats, and in rare cases bulls. This observation was made by J. Maweu (personal, March 28, 2008) a Christian respondent. As members of the community, they tried to understand the economic status of the people by applying empathy and kindness towards their clients. They are therefore friends to the people.

In the view of the researcher, given the contemporary hostile economy, any commodity selling at a friendlier prize will attract the eyes of many. This practice could therefore be a point of attraction of clients to diviners.

It is difficult to make a concrete analysis as to why a person is attracted to another because as the English saying goes "beauty is in the eyes of the beholder". Whatever attracts clients to diviners is best known to them and at times they may not be open enough to say it all. For example, the case of Beata who only admitted having visited several diviners but could not reveal the reasons for those visits. Nevertheless, a spoken word is often than not an indicator of an inner reality. What this researcher learned from different respondents was quite informative and substantive. The contribution from both Christian and non-Christian respondents revealed that those among them who were involved with diviners were people with genuine needs. For some of them the diviner was the final solution. With this in mind, in the following sub-section, we shall examine the repercussion of Christian involvement with diviners.

Consequences of involvement with diviners

The question on the impact of Christian involvement with diviners to fellow Christians was addressed to the Catholics only. This question enabled the researcher to assess whether the benefits sought for in the diviner by some, affected the faith of those around them in any way. From all the respondents, it was revealed that involvement with diviners by some members of the Church community affected the rest in various ways.

Some respondents pointed out that, experience of some Christians seeing their family members or neighbours and friends being helped by diviners created in them the desire to do the same. The Akamba say that he/she who spends time with the one affected by a rash will acquire the same rash (vai utinda na mukundu nda kunduke). An interview with M. Mutio, (personal communication, March 16, 2008) revealed that although all her children went to Church, this did not bar them from having rituals performed on them either by her or by other diviners. A certain nun (name withheld) shared with this writer that her own mother who is a traditional worshiper brought diviners to them for different rituals until she was in form three, a point at which she confronted one diviner and rejected his treatment. In the words of this nun, to this day, her mother continues to influence the rest of her sisters, brothers and their children. According to her, although some of them went to Church, more crucial was their influence over each other to act contrary to the demands of their Christian faith.

In a situation whereby majority of people are moving towards a given direction, it demands great courage, strength of mind and will to move contrary to the current. The researcher is in agreement that those Christians involved with diviners affected the rest greatly by way of influence. In this case it is worth noting that although these people may get to know the diviner through others, the motive remains the same, namely, to have their problems solved.

Those involved with diviners at times suffered guilt conscience because they knew the Church did not okay the practice. E.Muthoka (personal communication, March 6, 2008) a Church elder, had observed that some victims who previously had been active in the Church gave one reason or another for not attending services any more. This in turn affected the rest of the family members to the extent that some either stopped or became reluctant to go to Church too. The slackness of one person culminated in the back slide of many.

While it is true that the strength of one person can be the strength of another and the weakness of one the weakness of the other, it is still an individual's responsibility to stand firmly by one's star and walk ardently in the path of faith. Lack of conviction in one's faith may at times open chances for one to be waylaid by others by stronger folks.

The people involved with diviners teach others either directly or indirectly the traditional ways of managing difficult issues in life. All the diviners approached for information informed this writer that most of their Christian clients visited them at night. Syokwia (personal communication, March 8, 2008) said:

168

Many are the times when I am woken up by the sound of cars belonging to night visitors who preferred the night to the day. Many others wake me up in the wee hours of the night. When this happens, I know Christians have come and I must attend to them before dawn.

Night visits are meant to cover up a person's true identity whose life is in the real sense, dual in terms of faith. New clients learn from the old ones about the best time to visit without fear of being discovered. Perhaps these Christians have not yet heard the words of Jesus that, "Whatever is hidden will be brought out into the open, and whatever is covered up will be found and brought to light" (Luke 8: 17). The culture of living in the light should form the basic content for catechesis.

Another skill is that of walking to a diviner's house with a companion. During the field study, the researcher learned that, rarely do people visit a diviner without a companion. Men mostly take another man while women take another woman. Though no particular reason was given for this practice, it seems to have its basis in the ethical principles of the Akamba. Normally, one does not have to visit the diviner in the company of a relative and so to avoid sinister suspicions, a companion of the same sex is preferred unless otherwise in the case of relatives. J. Muthoka (personal communication, March 29, 2008) narrated to this researcher how as a young boy he accompanied his father to a diviner. In this case however, the study views the journey of a father and his son as a way of initiating the young man into the traditional ways of life. Although Muthoka thanked God that he found no treasure in the diviner, he however remarked that through such visits and sharing stories with those visiting diviners affected him in some way. What Muthoka puts across makes sense in that when people with common interests live together they easily influence each other.

Because of their alleged involvement with diviners, people who visit diviners often instill fear on fellow Christians. According to C. Kilonzo and N. Munyweiya (personal communication, March 29, 2008), both priests at Kasikeu parish, people were prone to the fear of those associated with diviners. This was due to the belief that such people possessed extra-ordinary powers that would harm others. A. Mang'ee (personal communication March 6, 2008) however viewed this fear from a different perspective. According to him, there were some Christians who used medicines from diviners to boost their business among others. Such people feared that interaction with those who were diviner friendly might lead to their disarmament. In relation to this, people known to be involved with diviners had a bad name in the Church community while others developed a negative attitude towards them. By their inclination towards the traditional ways of responding to crisis situations, these people unknowingly led others to sin.

Involvement with diviners by some members of the Church at times resulted in division. According to some respondents, at times it happens that in a Christian family some members believe in diviners while others do not. Those involved with diviners or vice versa may begin to intimidate, humiliate or undermine the others publicly causing a scandal and division in the Church and in Small Christian Communities at the same time. The researcher witnessed a situation whereby, a certain clan that outnumbered the rest in a certain Church Station was forced into the home of a diviner for traditional oaths (*ngata /ndundu*) something that affected the unity of this Station for quite some time. Christian unity can only be maintained if the members realized without doubt that there is only one body and one Spirit just as there is one hope to which God has called them (Ephesians 4: 4).

As noted earlier, in the traditional Akamba view, the diviner acts in the interest of the community, to create peace and to maintain harmony in the universe. This is in accord with Olupona's idea that diviners ameliorate, restore and reconcile estranged relationships (2000:87). However, although this still remains the focus of the diviner, it may not be fully at its best due to modern changes. In actual fact, among the Akamba today, the presence of the diviner has raised a lot of concern particularly among the Christians. Perhaps this explains why diviners have been viewed by some people as a source of division.

Some diviners advise their clients to make sure that they attend Church services without fail and secondly to receive the sacrament of reconciliation once done with the diviner. N. Kaleli, (personal communication, March 8, 2008), Syokwia (personal communication, March 8, 2008) and M. Mutio (personal communication, March 16 2008) were among those who revealed to the researcher of what they told their clients after taking them through the rituals. They did so because they knew the Church did not allow Christians to revert back to their traditions. Ndulu Particularly shared that while Christian clients needed her services, they nevertheless needed to maintain their faith. Both Ndulu and Syokwia were once Catholics and went through catechetical instructions before dodging baptism. For Christians who follow the instructions of these diviners, the Sacraments of Reconciliation and Eucharist become simple routines. Worse still, for the onlookers who are well aware of their movements, this can derail their faith too. At this point, although the victim may find consolation in the hands of the diviner, he/she stands torn between two conflicting systems; the traditional and the Christian religious systems.

It was further reported that, those Christians who involved themselves with diviners affected others' quality of participation in Church matters. One respondent remarked that some leaders were among the prime suspects of nocturnal activities. According to him, such leaders had no moral authority and commanded little respect from the Christians. As a result, some Small Christian Communities remained at the crawling stage while some other Christians remained nominal and passive in the Church. However, according to Mutisya, suspect leaders were demoted from their leadership seats once discovered.

While it is true that a section of the Akamba today have a very positive attitude towards diviners because of what they benefit from them, it is also true that another section does not experience their benefit and has nothing to do with them. This reality presents the two natural sides of life namely the positive and the negative. The positive side of diviners is fetched by those who consult them and have experienced growth, progress and harmony in their lives on consulting them or by using their advice and medicines. The negative side of diviners on the other hand is known to those who have been affected negatively by their activities either directly or indirectly through their family members or other people.

Methods of evangelization in the Catholic Diocese of Machakos

Due to the observed engagement of Christians with diviners in the Catholic Diocese of Machakos, the researcher set out to examine the methods of evangelization used by the teachers of faith and to determine whether they had contributed in any way to the mentioned practice or not. Although this question was addressed to the Christians and their leaders, it came out very strongly from the elderly Christians that the methods used in drawing people to the message of Christ had made a notable contribution to the Christian involvement with diviners. According to these Christians, the problem dates back to the missionary era. The discussion below highlights on the methods used by early missionary evangelizers and their possible link with Christian involvement with diviners.

Condemnation of traditional beliefs and practices

Missionaries looked upon African traditional beliefs and practices as evil and therefore to be disbanded. Condemnation of these practices was a skill applied by the missionaries as a way of ridding the people of their perceived evil practices such as *kilumi* dances, consultation of diviners for various needs and circumcision among others. Mugambi says, "On the scale of conversion, the foreign missionary gave himself 100% while the prospective convert was supposed to start at zero" (Mugambi, 1989: 8). This meant that what the missionary offered was the only viable content for salvation, and nothing of what the Africans already possessed. This same attitude has been referred to by Mbula (1982: 31) as already noted in chapter three.

In relation to the missionary attitude towards traditional practices of the people, most respondents reiterated that this attitude still existed even among

173

some African clergy todate. By their constant reference to the cultural beliefs and practices (kithio) in their homilies as anti the gospel message of Christ, it reaped mixed reactions from the Christians. According to M. Muthama (personal communication, March 14, 2008), condemnation of the people's traditional beliefs and practices, whether by missionaries or by local clergy, occasioned the reception of the gospel at face level while in reality people maintained harmony with their traditional beliefs and practices. Others who supported Muthama were Maweu, Kilavi and Kasuki. These Christians maintained that preaching against for example, the diviners' anti-witchcraft dose and other healing rituals were done even by the missionaries and yet these issues continued to manifest among the people. They reiterated that application of this same negative strategy and approach to preaching the gospel today contributed greatly to the people's stagnation in the activities of diviners.

Traditional beliefs and practices of a people define who they are, shape up their thinking and behavior in general. Given the observation by some of the respondents as just pointed out, it seems those involved in the work of evangelization in Machakos Diocese have at times applied strategies that instead of diminishing the problem of Christian involvement with diviners have created grounds for its silent bloom. While this is not the intention of these evangelizers it is also true that, condemnation of the the diviner or the people's traditional beliefs and practices does not exterminate them.

Establishment of Churches, Mission schools and hospitals
This strategy was applied by the missionaries in Ukambani as in other African States. Baur (1990: 43-46) implies that this effort was aimed at reaching out to

the people with the gospel message in ways that touched their real life situations. As already noted, there are over 52 parish churches each parish with not less than 10 prayer houses. This is a visible effort aimed at meeting for people's spiritual needs within their vicinity. For example, Kasikeu has a total of 16 prayer houses, Ikalaasa 14 prayer houses and Thatha 15 prayer houses (findings from Christian respondents). Likewise, the Diocese has several secondary and primary schools for example, Mbooni Girls, Muthetheni Girls and Misyani Girls. As already noted, the Diocese runs several health centers. Despite the establishment of these facilities, the study observed that proper strategies need to be put in place to ensure consistence in catechetical programs. Most Christian respondents were in agreement that these facilities were among the key tools through which the gospel message has been preached to the Akamba. However, some of them decried the lack of effective pastoral activities particularly in schools. They claimed that in some schools catechesis and pastoral classes were not operational. J. Muthoka (personal communication, March 9, 2008) from Kasikeu, a long serving catechist remarked that Catholic sponsored schools for example, were no longer strong avenues for the insertion of the Christian message to the learners. This was due to the heavy examination oriented curriculum resulting from the goals and demands of modern education. Another catechist R. Katee (personal communication, March 9, 2008) added that although schools were meant to build up learners integrally, no one dared to challenge learners whose parents or teachers were suspect witches due to fear of being accused of rumor monger y. One respondent, A. Muu (personal communication, March 19, 2008) related the example of one Christian teacher whose children could not attend school for some time because the whole family had to be treated by a diviner on suspicion that some one was bewitching them. No one challenged

175

their absenteeism. Because the problem of diviners is treated as a deeply cultural, the school administration may find it a delicate problem to discuss either with learners or their parents/guardians.

The above results indicate that physical facilities especially schools and hospitals were not reliable means of evangelization since they are mere structures. Although the school increases knowledge and hospitals take care of health challenges of the people, nevertheless, the inability of these institutions to address adequately the variety needs disturbing the human soul, mind and body increase the chances of some of them to consult diviners as traditional experts.

Listening carefully to these views, one would not miss realizing the hard ground on which leaders and agents of evangelization stand. Much as they would like to reach out to the people with the word of God a lot of blocks come their way. While this researcher rolls eyes on the lack of aggression by some leaders as expressed by some Christian respondents, it is worthy acknowledging efforts by local evangelizers in their pastoral activities. All the priests reached out for information shared a common view that both the Church, schools and hospitals needed to exert more energy on ensuring that their institutions reflected propagated the true faith of the Catholic Church.

Training of local agents of evangelization

Another method of evangelization that came to focus was the training of local clergy, religious and laity for evangelization. The Catholic Diocese of Machakos encourages young men and women to discern their vocations and to respond accordingly. As a result, the Diocese has at least two priests in each parish. There are also many sisters from the Diocese either working within or outside the diocese. The diocese also has a number of catechists working in various parishes. R. Mutisya (personal communication, March 15, 2008) the parish priest of Thatha strongly felt that this approach was bearing commendable fruits in adding to the number of qualified teachers of faith in the Diocese. Backed by Kilonzo and Munyweiya, these leaders saw their training and that of catechists as a step forward in the effort to promote Christian faith in the Diocese. These views were countered by some Christian respondents who felt that despite their training, these leaders were not aggressive enough in addressing the issue of Christian involvement with diviners in the Diocese hence its persistence. S. Mwinzi (personal communication, March 7, 2008) further argued that some of the catechists and some other Church leaders also fell prey to the diviners' activities raising questions on their credibility. For example, Emangu, once leader of a Small Christian Community was at one time involved with diviners until the community members decided to replace her (Observation by the researcher). Emangu not being the only case of a leader who consulted diviners, Christian respondents strongly felt that, having leaders who did not portray the right image was a soft ground for the fall of their subjects. The researcher concurs with this view and re comments faith renewal courses and workshops for prospective leaders before undertaking any leadership task in the Church.

Call to Christian charity

As a method of evangelization, the Catholic Diocese of Machakos preaches the gospel of Christian charity. According to a number of Christian respondents, since the replacement of missionaries by local clergy, there has been a complete turn of events whereby, instead of the Church supporting the

177

Christian community with material needs such as food, money and even clothing as the missionaries did, she is now on the receiving end. S. Mwanthi (personal communication, March 20, 2008) and Malinda (personal communication, March 28, 2008) shared similar opinion that there were some people who due to poverty sought a way forward from diviners. Some other Christians such as, U. Ndolo (personal communication, March8, 2008), J. Mutala (personal communication, March 17, 2008) and C. Mutiso (personal communication, March 17, 2008) observed that failure of the Church to meet the material needs of its members had exposed some poor people to the temptation of seeking solution to their problems from diviners. Another respondent P. Kimomo, (personal communication, March 6, 2008) asserted that some patients did not even call for a priest because they could not afford the stipulated amount as stipend and transport for the Priest hence endangering the state of their faith. One priest (name withheld) who was asked by this writer to comment on Kimomo's claim confirmed that very few patients called for anointing or even healthy Christians for the celebration of the Eucharist in their homes or in the Small Christian Communities.

This scenario indicates that to a certain extent, faith and material well being are related. Perhaps this is why James says "suppose there were brothers or sisters who need clothes and do not have enough to eat. What good is there in your saying to them, "God bless you! Keep you warm and eat well!" if you do not give them the necessities of life?" (2: 15-16). Although one of the respondents (Ruth Malinda) stressed that some Christians resulted to diviners because of poverty related challenges that were not addressed by the Church, this researcher however, does not support the idea of dishing out material things as a way of preaching the gospel unless one is in dire need. This kind of a practice promotes redundancy. Instead, both sides should do their best to become as self reliant as possible in terms of food, clothing and shelter without loading one another with unnecessary burdens.

General observations

The diviner's homestead

During interviews with diviners, the researcher observed several things that are worthy mentioning. In total, six diviners were visited, five women and one man. It was quite striking to this writer that in all the homes visited, there were no lockable gates. The compounds were simply fenced. The researcher realized that their homes had no gates as a sign of welcome to all who wished to visit them at any hour of the day or night.

Another observation was that these diviners lived under more or less the same house conditions. One of them had a grass thatched house while the other five had iron sheet roofed houses. Out of the six diviners, only one had a cemented floor which was not swept. The key point here is that, the houses of all the diviners visited were in poor condition and everything in these houses portrayed poverty. One respondent M. Kasuki (personal communication, March 29, 2008) told the researcher that this condition was intentional. It was not that diviners could not afford better housing but that they preferred to live under simple house structures. He explained that the spirits of the people from whom the powers had been inherited were more familiar with such house conditions and not modern houses. Secondly, it was explained that these diviners had to remain in the traditional state as a continuation of the Akamba traditional culture that was simple and natural. Another respondent A. Maweu (personal communication, March 28, 2008) explained that diviners segregated themselves so as to hide what is in them and by so doing remained ignorant of the modern world around them. This study agrees with many of the reasons given by different respondents as to why diviners looked poor. For sure diviners have money and by the nature of their ministry amass a lot of wealth in terms of goats and cows. Some of them did mention to the researcher that they had educated all their children through their work.

Further observation was that inside the house of each instrumental diviner, there were some long drums hanging on the wall at some corner. According to the diviners, the inauguration ceremony was carried out through music and dance (kilumi) in dedication to the ancestral spirit that had laid hands on the new initiate. As a requirement, these dances must be performed for the spirits to dance from time to time as this pleased them greatly. During the dance, some spirits possessed the dancers, released messages to them and made their requests. For this reason, if a particular diviner worked with one spirit, one drum would be found in her home. For example, Ndulu Kithuka had four drums meaning that she worked under the instructions of four different spirits. Among those she mentioned were her deceased grandfather and her late husband's brother. Syokwia had two drums, Vata two and Mutio two. Ndulu Kaleli did not expose hers while Makula had none. In the case of Ndulu, she simply mentioned that she had more instruments in her keeping including the drums but did not show them to us. As for Makula, the inauguration ceremony was carried out in another diviner's home so he did not acquire his own drums. This does not however hamper his work in any way. Along with this, it is important to realize that diviners who only performed rituals did not keep drums and only in very rare cases that a dance would be held in their houses.

In some of the houses, there were assorted objects that could not easily be identified. For example, in the house of Ndulu Kaleli there was an ostrich egg hanging at the entrance of the consultation room.

Figure 6: An ostrich egg in Ndulu Kaleli's house

This Ostrich egg is placed strategically at the entrance of the house of Ndulu Kaleli. She refused to unveil to the researcher the secret behind the egg. As she carries out the divination, clients face the direction of this egg. Photo by research assistant, March, 2008

According to M. Kasuki (personal communication, March 29, 2008), the use of this type of Ostrich egg is a common practice among diviners. The Akamba refer to it as *kuumbwa mavinya* (to concentrate the powers). When asked by the researcher's assistant what it was, the diviner simply said it was for her work and would not discuss it any further. The researcher would have thought it was an object of power for attracting customers.

In this same house, there was a portrait of Jesus hanging on the cross. This picture was suspended on the wall of the inner room where consultation with Christians took place. When asked why she kept a Christian picture in her house yet she did not believe in Christ she said that it had nothing to do with her. It was meant for the Christians who believed in him. Such a picture would surely make a Christian feel at home. Observation by the researcher was that although the picture resembled the calvary scenario, it was far from it. Jesus would not be agonizing from the cross while at the same time standing below it. It was a misleading picture reflecting the spirit world.

Figure 7: A Christian portrait in Ndulu Kaleli's house

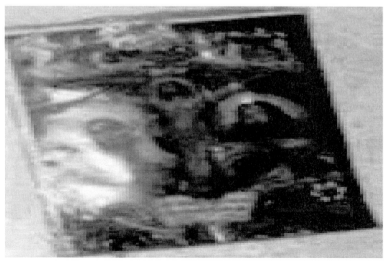

Photo by research assistant, March, 2008
This picture is unique as can be noticed from the photo. It is placed on the
wall in the second room. According to her, it is from this room where she
attends to Christian clients. At the back of this room is an exit door, a sign of
privacy for her clients.

Feathers of chickens and animal skins were also observed in some homes.
Other objects spotted were sea shells and stone like objects. They appeared to
this writer like sea collections but discussion about them was not fruitful.

It was further observed that all the women diviners visited possessed an
accordion, a divination bow and a calabash, as well as the diviner's gourd and
pebbles. It was discovered that a cross like mark in black color appeared on
top of the gourd and calabash. All the diviners simply said that this was the
diviners' identity mark (niw'o uvano wa mundu mue).

Dressing

It was observed that diviners had a special dress code. Although all the
diviners seemed to have the same kind of attire, some differences were
observed. Below is an example of a diviner in official outfit.

Figure 8: An example of a diviner's dress code

photo by the researcher, March, 2008

The above photo shows Ndulu Kaleli dressed for a divination session on request by the researcher and her assistant. According to her each of the cloth is significant to the role she plays as a diviner. For example, blue is for the family Shepherd (muithi) while red is for the spirits with whom she works. According to her neighbours, she is widely consulted.

Different diviners wore rings on one finger. They explained to this researcher that the rings belonged to the owner of the work. The rings bound them to cooperate with the particular spirits to whom they had vowed to serve devoutly and as directed.

General approach to clients

The researcher experienced warmth, openness and freedom from diviners. They were all very welcoming. During interviews they showed readiness and freedom to share their story which proved to the researcher that diviners were not ashamed or sorry to exist. They actually felt needed and wanted in society. In this connection, they are never in a hurry because they say it would interfere with the results of their divination. However, one major observation made was that none of them talked of food. Even those we spent about two hours with, there was no mention of food. To this writer, this could not be lack of hospitality but a deep sense of responsibility. They were on business and therefore no time for entertainment. Another reason why diviners may not offer food or drink to customers could be a way of protecting themselves from people's blame in case a client developed complications after a meal. Because they are the manufacturers of different medicines, should some one eat or drink from them and develop complications they would have to bear the blame. Thirdly, the researcher came to understand that some clients were in a hurry to finish with them and move away before they were noticed. Finally, since diviners received many customers it would be quite expensive to provide daily meals.

High sense of commitment to duty and submission to authority

Direct contact with diviners during visits in their homes revealed that they were very conscious of their work. All those observed revealed a great sense of responsibility, deep understanding of their ministry and high level commitment to the word and directive of the spirits. This knowledge was arrived at as the researcher watched them dress at our request. They each took their time and placed each item at its rightful place. Some of the items were animal skins, the gourd and the bow. N. Kaleli (personal communication, March 8, 2008) remarked "Let me do it the right way. I do not want to be beaten for making some one's work a show" Syokwia (personal communication, March 8, 2008) on her part could not touch the official clothes without some form of payment. This she said was a directive from her angel.

Apart from commitment to their work as diviners, they also engaged in normal money generating activities such as, trade and farming. They performed their routine house hold duties such as, cooking, fetching firewood and water.

Assertive, competent and confident
The researcher noted in each diviner the virtue of self confidence and assertiveness. They were not afraid to speak out their convictions. When they did it, it was done with respect. They narrated their self perceived roles as diviners in a flow of words. None of them portrayed weakness or inability to perform a ritual or to fulfill a client's need. Each one of them saw and presented him/herself as the most skilled hence winning the confidence of their clients. One of the diviners interviewed related how she enabled a scared client to relax and narrate his story by relating to him the dream she had had the previous night about his coming. Once someone trusts the other, the outcomes are also acceptable and there is no cause for doubt. Due to the personal conviction of their call, diviners are very committed to their work. In the contemporary society, some people place the coat on the chair to indicate their presence as they move to other businesses but not a diviner. On the contrary, a diviner will sit waiting on his/her clients until all is done. Generally their disposition is a source of challenge to all who see them and may act as a

point of attraction to those around them.

Example of a divination session

The researcher did not have the opportunity to observe the diviner at a very close range although she could still see from a distance what was being done. However, communication between her and the clients could be heard, the rattling gourd, the tickling of the bow and the accordion music. We could see the clients clearly as they sat directly to us and the door was open. Some two ladies had gone to consult the diviner over a sick child. Before the session commenced, there were some low tone conversations that could not be heard. After all the preliminary preparations and arrangement of the tools on a goat skin, the diviner began by calling on the client to place the consultation fee on the hide which was promptly done. Since there was no negotiation about this, the observer thought the clients knew of the required fee. The diviner removed some pebbles from the gourd placing them gently on the animal skin. It was as though she was trying to establish the number of pebbles in the gourd. After a while she fixed the bow and began playing it. The tickling of the bow and calabash was accompanied by some kind of singing and talking at the same time. Although this researcher could not follow everything, what came out clearly was the invitation of the spirits from various destinations to the session in order to reveal the truth.

The gourd followed after the bow. She began by shaking it severally after which she gently let out the pebbles on the skin. Three pebbles came out and she exclaimed "It is within the family. Look! Here they are, three of them meaning that you know the problem already!

Diviner - Tell me how this child was born

Client -   With some difficulties

Diviner - What difficulties?

Client - Prolonged labour pains and after birth the child took long to cry

Diviner - What happened to the placenta?

Client - It was buried behind the house

Diviner - Was there a ceremony carried out afterwards?

Client – No

Diviner -This is where you went wrong, the family shepherd (Muithi) needed to be appeased. Difficult labour and the subsequent health problems signify that something was not done in the right way.

Client - What then can be done?

Diviner - Three things need to be done. A goat has to be sacrificed in the name of this child and some piece of its skin placed on the wrist (kwikiwa kikonde), the shepherd's clothe has to be bought for the child (ngua ya muithi). This ceremony acts as an introduction of the child to the guardian of the family. Thirdly, the original birth place of the child has to be revisited and some blood (of a goat) and beer libations offered to the ancestors.

The diviner expressed readiness to accomplish the necessary rituals once the family was ready with everything. The issue of payment was not discussed. Observation of the clients revealed reverence for the diviner and all that she spoke. This could be seen from the attentive listening true that divination is time consuming, calls for long sitting hours, demands a lot of accorded the diviner by the two women who sat quietly facing her. At one point the diviner did as though to massage the child and said, "uu nuvitanu" (this is the result of rejection of a necessary custom). This statement was an emphasis to what had already been prescribed to the two women.

For the second time the diviner went into silence then we heard very sweet sounding music of the accordion. This went on for some time after which she began to rattle the gourd once again, producing some funny sounds amidst yawning which the researcher could not comprehend. At some point it was like she was in dialogue with someone because she severally responded "ii ni w'o" (Yes! It is true). She then counted the number of pebbles up to seven and turned to her clients saying "iyoniei, muonza u mwai na mwithianu" (see yourselves here is seven, the deadly number). Seven pebbles are associated with witchcraft. This was the reason why the diviner showed them to the clients. After some discussion with the child's mother the conclusion was that the mid-wife who is also the person that buried the placenta had evil eyes and that this had also affected the child's health. After this observation we left the compound.

From the above divination process, the researcher realized that in divination the client was a very key person. Although the diviner was the first to mention the possible causes to the problem, a conclusion was arrived at after some dialogue with the client. The diviner at this point acted not only as a discerner but also as an interpreter of cultural issues as observed by Rudolph among the Batammaliba of Togo (in Peek, 1991: 73). This study also realized that diviners used a lot of psychology and wisdom in dealing with clients. Vata exercised a lot of patience, listened actively to her clients and maintained a calm atmosphere throughout the session. Apart from these natural aids applied by the diviner, she also appealed to the help of spiritual powers in discerning the problem at hand. From the researcher's observation, this divine appeal maximized the clients' confidence in the final results of the entire process.

189

During interviews with different respondents including Christians, it became evident that the Akamba considered diviners as mystics because of their ability to enter into communication with spiritual beings. According to the results of this study, when the Akamba, including Christians visit diviners, it is because they believe in the power of the departed to understand and to provide solutions to their problems. The diviner is therefore consulted as a mediator.

Emerging Issues

Several issues related to this study, though not directly reflected in the study questions came up during the field research. These are:

Divination as a call in the traditional setting

N. Kaleli (personal communication, March 8, 2008) is one diviner who viewed herself as equally called to serve the community in a special way. She said "Nyie na Muvea nundu umwe. Kila umwe etitwe athukume andu ma Ngai kwa nzia ya mwanya na yi kivathukanio" (between me and a Priest there is no difference because each of us is called to serve God's people in a special and unique way). She was categorical that she would never convert to Christianity as this would amount to betrayal of her ancestral career. She further argued that the Church did not understand in depth the Akamba culture and was therefore ignorant of many things without which a Mukamba would not experience lasting harmony with self, others and the spiritual world. According to her this impediment on the side of the Church necessitated the continued intervention of diviners in solving issues that the Church ignored. For this reason she was deeply convinced that diviners were put in place by God to bridge in this gap for a harmonious living.

In support of divination as a serious call in the traditional Kamba community, K. Mukala (personal communication, March 14, 2008) narrated to the researcher, the story of a woman who surrendered the tools of her mother in-law to a Priest after her death. The deceased woman diviner had already mentioned her own sister as the one to inherit her tools and to continue with her mission. Three days after the tools were burnt by the Priest, the woman who handed them over to him died. According to Kitulya, the tools of a diviner affirm a special call that should not be interfered with. Traditionally if the tools are not inherited after the death of a diviner they should not be removed from the house till it falls and its contents are consumed by ants. This incident served as a lesson to the priest about the seriousness of traditional matters. Despite the need to evangelize to people everywhere, care has to be taken to understand and to respect the other religion.

There are specific signs and initiation ceremonies for diviners

M. Musau (personal communication, March 16, 2008) narrated how she suffered a mysterious disease immediately after marriage. She experienced persistent attacks of headache, vomiting blood and general malaise. She also stayed long without conceiving and yet in all these, nothing organic was diagnosed in the hospital. It was only after she accepted to inherit the divination powers of her grandfather that she regained her health and everything turned fruitful for her. During the initiation ceremony she received a divination gourd with pebbles, the diviner's bow and a calabash, a white piece of cloth with red strips (for the owner of the work), a black cap and a red cloth (demanded by her grandfather as divination uniform).

Another diviner Ndulu Kaleli (8th March, 2008) shared with this researcher that she inherited her powers from her grandmother Nyiva. She was therefore working with her and another family elder Ndunda. She knew them because they appeared to her in a dream and took her to the forest, and showed her the herbs she would use for her work. They still guide her to date, she says. Ndulu who claims she was born with two pebbles in her navel also confirmed that she later vomited them and were still in her divination gourd. After marriage, she developed complications and could not eat before taking some tobacco. Only after she was initiated did she regain her full health. During the initiation ceremony she was handed the following: 2 divination bows and 2 calabashes, 2 divination gourds, an animal skin, a necklace, a blue cloth with red and white strips demanded by her grandmother's mother, a red cloth for *Kathambi* (the spirit of the heavens), a black dress for *Veke* (a certain spirit who assists in divination), a red cloth similar to that of *Kathambi* for placing on top of the divination skin, a mirror for her work, a cap with many buttons (for the soldiers- spirits who act as guardians) a bell (mbwii or ndilili) and the diviner's basket (*kathango* made of *muumo* fibre or sisal).

The above tools and clothes handed to this diviner during the inauguration ceremony must all be used at the same time during a divination session, and in accordance with the original instructions. This is because if one item that was once used by the one from whom powers were inherited, the divination session may not progress smoothly due to disturbance from some of these spirits.

Syokwia (personal communication March 8, 2008) reported to the researcher that she was born with difficulties. As a young girl she developed the gift of clairvoyance and all members of the family confirmed to her that she had a special call to become a diviner. She inherited her grandfather's powers of a diviner and received it with openness and joy. For the inauguration ceremony, she said many goats were slaughtered and libations of blood and beer offered. She also received the divination gourd with pebbles, the divination bow and calabash, an accordion, a red cap with a black lining (as the one worn by her grand mother the diviner), a black piece of cloth with red strips (suka wa mwiitu mulaika- for the lady angel), a white piece of cloth with red strips (suka wa muithi- for the shepherd), a second white piece of cloth with red strips (suka wa muthiani- for the prophet). In addition she received *kilumi* drums.

The above items are the same as those that were used by her grandmother. By wearing the same attire as her grandmother from whom she inherited the powers is a sign of continuation of a family charisma. Just like in the case of other diviners referred to in this dissertation, special clothing is dictated by the governing spirit, the one from whom the powers of divination have been inherited. According to Syokwia, she may miss out any other clothing during her divination but not that of the lady angel. She is the governing spirit in all her sessions.

N. Kithuka (personal communication, March 26, 2008) told of her rainbow experience. As a young girl in school the rainbow would stop right in front of her after which she would fall and be taken home. At night a voice kept asking her to leave school which she finally did. After some time she got married. A few months later she was expectant but soon after developed complications. She was referred to Kenyatta National Hospital where although doctors could

193

see the pregnancy they would not locate the fetus and this lasted six months. It was at this point that a diviner was consulted who declared that *kilumi* dance was needed and some special clothing identified as, *wanyua* (a necklace with small beads of mixed colors) and *kanyiki* (a black piece of cloth). Although the dances were carried both at her parents and marital homes, she continued to resist being initiated into divination until she gave birth to her third child. Immediately after this delivery, she went dumb true that divination is time consuming, calls for long sitting hours, demands a lot of; the breasts produced no milk and she could not hold the baby. With this experience she finally surrendered and the inauguration ceremony was carried out after which she became a healthy woman. Ten goats were slaughtered, beer and blood libations offered and the gift of tobacco and divination tools handed to her officially. She works with four different spirits with each presented in her house by a *kilumi* drum. Special tools, clothes and ornaments given: A watch and a ring shown to her in a dream by her husband's brother, a necklace in honor of the owner of the work, a black cloth, four drums repr true that divination is time consuming, calls for long sitting hours, demands a lot ofesenting the four spirits at work with her, a bungle from her grandfather from whom she inherited the powers, an accordion, five calabashes, two divination bows, a divination true that divination is time consuming, calls for long sitting hours, demands a lot of gourd, pebbles and some sea shells.

Initiation done after marriage

During the field study it emerged that initiation to divination only takes place after marriage. The study further established that the most common and acceptable form of divination was by inheritance from one's family. In the case of women, it is the other diviners who collect the divination tools from her father's home. The initiation ceremony begins there and ends at the marital home. It involves the sacrifice of cows, libations of blood, milk and beer as well as different foods particularly finger millet meal mixed with ghee or milk. Through this ceremony, the person is dedicated to the spirits behind her call through a clothing ceremony as already noted. Tobacco is also given to the initiate in a small gourd (kiangi). One is to partake of it in the name of the spirits one is dedicated to since old people enjoyed and still enjoy tobacco.

More women diviners than men

The study revealed that there were more women diviners than men among the Akamba. It was also revealed that women were more of gourd diviners than ritual diviners while there were more men in the ritual category. From the observation of the researcher, it is true that divination is time consuming, calls for long sitting hours, demands a lot of patience, keen listening, understanding, intuition, empathy and kindness among other virtues. These virtues are more common in women than in men hence the reason for their popularity. Traditionally, the Akamba women held private duties, domestic in nature meaning their movement out of the home was limited. On the contrary, men engaged in activities that demanded movement to long distances in search of pasture and large clan meetings among others. Ritual divination calls for a lot of movement as one endeavors to reach out to clients in their homes and business premises something that naturally favours men. Perhaps another explanation would be that the Akamba women are more susceptible to spirit possession during the *kilumi* dances than men. This is because this dance is exclusively for women although some men still enjoy it for example, Mulili from Ngomano.

Diviners' attitude to the Church

The diviners interviewed shared a common argument that worship does not necessarily have to be carried out in a Church. All of them were convinced that their homes were sufficient centers of worship. Some of them wanted to become Christians before they were initiated. Mutio was a member of the African Inland Church and was known by the name Alice. She admitted to the researcher that her spirit, the owner of the work would not allow her into the Church. That is why she always fell sick on the week of baptism. According to her she cannot go to Church because it would be against her faith and the faith of those she works.

Syokwia belonged to the Catholic Church but never made it for baptism. According to her, she forced herself to the Church against the will of her people (spirits) and was always knocked down at the Church entrance forcing her to go back home. Finally a missionary priest in-charge of the Parish then asked her to remain at home after putting a Rosary on her neck. When she began her work as a diviner, she kept it away to avoid causing confusion among the Christians she says, and secondly to avoid ambiguity in her work.

Ndulu Kaleli had a similar experience to share. As a former Catholic, she went to Church and attended catechism but something always blocked her from baptism. Although the parish priest prayed with her several times there was no breakthrough. When she finally accepted initiation into divination it was now clear to her that the Church was not the right place for her. By the time the researcher reached out to her for interview, four Masses had been offered in her home in a bid to have her converted. To the surprise of this generous priest, at the fourth Mass she asked him to keep off and set her free to follow her career and way of worship. Ndulu retorted that the Church and the diviner were apart from each other and therefore each should keep to its way without undermining the other. She said this in reaction to attempts by the priests to persuade her to join the Church. To crown her words, she further claimed to have authorized her family members that after her death, none of her tools should be taken to the Church for whatever purpose. Ndulu remarked to the interviewee that she wanted to remain focused and uninfluenced in her work. In fact at one point the researcher asked her if she would ever think of returning to the Church and she retorted "Do you also want to preach to me? Do not waste your time trying it"

In relation to the Church, this study found out that, diviners would neither have Christian names nor receive any of the sacraments. They did not want to have their homes blest, but gave Sunday offertory contributions to their children with no problem and at the same time encouraged them to go to Church. Mutio and Ndulu Kaleli openly told the researcher that they would not like to block any one from following their desired faith. At this point the researcher asked Ndulu if by attending to Christians they were not interfering with their faith. In response she charged that it was actually the Christians who went to her home in search of her assistance. According to her, it would be wrong and against her call to turn away a client on the basis of faith. In further defense of her career, she informed the researcher that she always reminded her Christian clients to go for confession after fulfilling all the prescribed rituals and to remain faithful in Church attendance. This means that as a diviner she knew too well that what she led Christians through was incompatible with their faith. According to this lady, it was not money that motivated her into the career bu the desire to promote life.

The diviner's herbal medicine

The researcher got to learn that the herbal medicine of a diviner was more than herbs. M. Kasuki (personal communication, March 29, 2008), a staunch Catholic born with seven pebbles who escaped narrowly from becoming a diviner by entering the seminary received substantial experience from his grandfather who was a diviner. According to Kasuki the diviner's medicine has to undergo a ritual to render it powerful. Diviners refer to the ritual as *kuthyuuwa muti*. Even poisonous plants such as *kilyambiti*, the most poisonous plant in Ukambani are taken through the same ritual to remove the poison. To a diviner therefore, there is nothing poisonous. This was confirmed by Makula, a ritual diviner who followed the same procedure for his cleansing and oral medicines.

Christian attitude towards bi-religious practices

By sharing with Christian respondents, it came out clearly that some Christians suffered guilty conscience due to their interaction with diviners while others remained unaffected, received the Holy Eucharist as usual even without receiving the sacrament of reconciliation, assumed leadership roles in the Church and in the Small Christian Communities. A respondent who declined to be named gave the example of her mother in-law who visited diviners every now and then, and yet in the Church she was among the high profile Christians. The respondents remarked that today there is not much reverence of the Church among those Christians who consult diviners as compared to earlier days when people would stay away from the sacraments until they sorted themselves out. According to them, many Christians today are not serious with their faith.

A ceremonial goat (Mbui ya muthyuukyo)

This is a goat that is taken round a particular village once a year. The traditional elders in every region approach one of them for a sacrificial goat. The one donating the goat has to do it willingly. This ritual is also a sign of self surrender to God in obedience to the ancestors. This takes place before the long rains commence around September. This long journey begins at 5 a.m or even earlier with four elders taking the goat along with them. At the end of the journey, the goat is slaughtered but after being suffocated and blood scooped for libation. Some of the meat is offered to the spirits and the rest is roasted and shared among those present. The skin is shared among the four elders who hang it at their gates on their return home. At times they carry the contents of the large intestines which are either mixed with water or food for use in the family for protection. According to M.Kituli (personal communication, March 7, 2008), the purpose of this journey with a goat is to beseech God and all the spirits to protect the particular village from illness and evil in general. During the preliminary plans, the diviner is consulted in order to predict on which shrine the goat should be slaughtered.

Registration of diviners

From the Government officials that participated in the study it was revealed that majority of diviners were registered as traditional herbalists. Chief Joseph Ngui a Christian of Thatha parish mentioned that apart from being registered as traditional practitioners, they had an organization and an office. This same observation was made by Ngundo (2001) in her study among the Akamba of Muthetheni. In fact all diviners are supposed to come out in the open for registration for their own security. Cases have been reported of patients dying, becoming worse or conditions deteriorating after visiting a diviner. In case of such rare eventualities, a registered diviner cannot be accused of being involved in an illegal practice. When we went to the home of Mutio she was very nervous and uncomfortable with us. She interrogated us thoroughly to know the motive of our research. Finally she confessed that she feared we were Government people since she was not a registered practitioner. Participants in witchcraft eradication rituals *Ngata/Ndundu* are also served with certificates in some cases to avoid being forced back to the ritual. Only a registered diviner can carry out this ceremony and issue certificates to participants.

Hurdles of the study

It was a tough road to tread but we finally got there. Despite the commendable cooperation from the respondents, there were some difficulties experienced. The first challenge was the long distant walks that we had to endure. Most places were not accessible by car forcing us to walk through challenging paths and bushes.

Another challenge faced was lack of complete openness by some diviners. While the researcher greatly appreciates their warm welcome and long hours of sharing, it is also worth pointing out that there was a depth that we could not penetrate. For example, Syokwia told us plainly that she was only exposing to us some of her working tools and not everything. The reasons for this limit were that the owner of the work may think she is making a show of what is sacred to them. The same was experienced with Ndulu Kaleli who would not open up about some objects in her keeping such as the ostrich egg. She also refrained from letting us into the room where she kept her tools. Mutio's case was not exceptional either.

There were moments when some of the diviners stared hard at the researcher without a word. At time they ignored questions posed to them. For this reason, although the desired information from diviners was gathered, there were some details the researcher wished to know but could not have a break through. At times when they sensed we were getting into matters of faith there was a tendency of self defense. As the interviews proceeded, Ndulu Kaleli cautioned that matters of faith should not be discussed and so it became difficult to talk about her relationship with God and spirits as a diviner. This was an indication that there were some things she kept secret and would not allow any penetration.

Christians too posed another challenge to the researcher. When approached for information, at the first instant, none admitted having had any association with diviners. Only with time did some begin to open up to this reality. By the end of the study although Christian respondents still answered the questions posed at them positively, the researcher felt that they could have done better than that.

Conclusion

It is quite interesting to be speaking of the strength of a traditional specialist (a diviner) after more than a century of civilization in Africa. It is also more than hundred years now since the gospel reached the African continent. In the Akamba traditional setting, the diviner has been a key consultant and more often than not, a healer. All diviners are strict adherents of traditional religion and are therefore its custodians. However, it is worthy noting that their numbers have decreased significantly since the introduction of Christianity and modern education. This decrease can further be explained by the fact that diviners were never young people and so many of them have died. In fact those visited were between fifty five and seventy five years old. Nevertheless, despite the reduced numbers, we realize that the work of diviners has continued to thrive. The fact that people move for distances in search of them is an indication that these specialists are still valued in the community. The researcher and her assistants went through this experience. For example, to reach Mutio's home it was such a weary journey of about an hour through bushes. The same case applied to Makula where we had to hire some transport.

It is also apparent that today very few young people are interested in the career which makes inheritance difficult. On inquiry about the future of their work, all the diviners were optimistic that their tools would not be laid down after their death. They confidently asserted "Divination among the Akamba will never end, it is there to stay because it is a God given ministry". One of the sons of Ndulu Kaleli who is in his late 30s and a Christian firmly refuted the idea that the Akamba form of divination will ever come to an end.

The researcher has observed that the Akamba traditional diviners charged moderately as discussed earlier in this chapter hence attracting many customers. However, according to one of the diviners, their charges can fall or rise depending on the diviner's judgment of the client's economic status. On the whole, the findings of this study were that the Akamba of today including Christians were still attracted to the diviner. This was heightened by the experience of suffering in human life which manifests itself in various forms.

CHAPTER SIX: THE DIVINER AS A CHALLENGE TO CHRISTIAN FAITH

Introduction

The purpose of this study was to investigate the relevance of the Akamba diviner in contemporary Akamba community with reference to the Catholic Diocese of Machakos. The choice of the topic was inspired by the researcher's observation that despite many years of evangelization among the Akamba, the diviner still maintained his traditional role among the people. The utmost concern of this book is to promote deeper and a more integrated Christian faith not only among the Christians of the Catholic diocese of Machakos but for the entire Christian community.

During the study, it became apparent that many people sought consolation from diviners in time of crisis. In a funeral Mass (30th May, 2008), Nzioka, the Parish Priest of Ikalaasa exerted further confirmation to this in his homily. As part of his preaching, he sought to know if any of the Christians present had visited a diviner. Five Christians acknowledged by putting up their hands while a section faced down and the rest laughed. Father's conclusion was that he was sure the number of those who had visited diviners was higher than those who owned up. He further generalized that there were very few Christians who lived up to the ideal Christian values.

The study further revealed that the diviner was still valued by many of the Akamba as a cultural specialist. Respondents stated that from a cultural point of view, the Akamba diviner was a wisdom figure in the community. When people were faced with dilemma and wanted to understand the mystery surrounding their lives, the most knowledgeable person to approach was a diviner. This is because of the existing notion that diviners understood better the Akamba world view. In this respect, the study found out that the Akamba diviners were revered as mediators between the physical and the spiritual world, as counselors, prophets and depositories of extra-ordinary powers that enabled them to diagnose disease and other disturbing situations thereby providing possible solutions to daily life challenges.

As traditional specialists, it was revealed that diviners dealt with a variety of problems. Among these were problems that could only be well explained from a cultural point of view such as, broken taboos, curses, traditional oaths and witchcraft. Respondents described these cases as real cultural dilemmas that needed the intervention of higher powers to bestow those affected to normalcy.

The diviners' approach to human suffering is integral. The study found out that, diviners attributed various human afflictions to a variety of causes ranging from organic to spiritual and social. Even when the cause of a disease was clearly organic, the diviner went further to establish why the particular person was affected and not any other. The study found out that, nearly in every case of human suffering among the Akamba, the diviner would either prescribe herbs, offering of sacrifice to the offended spirit, some kind of clothing and ritual cleansing in accordance with the nature of the problem or a combination of two or more of these remedies. This cultural approach to disease and healing enabled the diviner to eliminate all culturally known possible causes to human suffering. Where the diviner was unable to find a concrete explanation to something, he/she declared for example, a disease or sickness as originating from God (uwau wa Ngai). What is from God has no human cure and can either culminate in the death or cure of the victim as per God's wish.

At the time of divination, diviners interchanged different tools. Some commonly used tools are a divination bow with a calabash, an accordion and a small gourd. The researcher observed that, before handling the working tools, special dressing was necessary to put the session at its rightful place. The findings of this study were that the specific dressing observed by each diviner was in accordance with the instructions of partner spirit/spirits. According to diviners, familiar spirits took control over them during a divination session to influence the outcomes of the process.

During this study, the researcher came to the awareness that diviners attracted a lot of clients due to their ability to provide prompt solutions to clients' problems. Respondents informed the researcher that the client was always part of the final solution. In relation to this, the researcher learned that in very rare cases would a diviner not provide an answer to a client's problem. One diviner referred to it as "divination silence" meaning there is no response from the working spirits. If this did happen, the diviner would advice the client to consult another diviner of choice for a second opinion.

The study further revealed that, the Christian attitude towards most traditional practices and beliefs as well as evangelization strategies applied in the Diocese paved way to Christian deviation from their faith and led them back to their traditional roots. Christian respondents pointed to poor initiation of converts to Christian faith, at times done by untrained catechists and other poorly trained teachers of faith. They also cited lack of on-going faith formation which was blamed for exposing vulnerable Christians to the danger of being influenced to the activities of the diviner. Further indications were that, those involved in the work of faith formation still portrayed a negative image of diviners and all that surrounded them causing dissension between those who believed and those who did not believe in the activities of these traditional specialists.

Facing the reality

In the contemporary Akamba community the diviner is widely viewed and accepted as a traditional specialist. The Akamba in the traditional setting look to the wisdom, skill and power of the diviner for a continued harmonious living among humans, humans and the entire creation and between humans and the spiritual world. To achieve these, the traditional elders and traditional worshipers share the responsibility of consulting with diviners from time to time and to perform the necessary ceremonies and rituals as directed.

There is something distinct about the Akamba diviners. In the first place, these people identify themselves with spiritual beings. These may be their own ancestral spirits, spirits of other diviners or spirits of people unknown to them but who introduce themselves to them through dreams. In most cases, diviners work with spirits whom they can call by name. In rare cases, diviners would conjure spirits in general for assistance. The researcher heard a diviner call on spirits from the forest and the sea during a divination session. These experiences strengthen the conclusion by this researcher that diviners have in them something beyond the ordinary people.

Secondly, as mystics, it is believed that they possess supernatural powers either tapped from the universe or powers of the spiritual beings under whose influence the diviner operates. The question of possession of supernatural powers by human beings has often been met with suspicion if not rejection yet, it is not impossible for people to have these powers. Jesus himself possessed supernatural powers and his followers as well. In 2006 this researcher participated in a day of prayer facilitated by J. Baptist Bashobora. During one of his inputs, some two sisters walked to the field with four men carrying a paralyzed woman whom they laid close to my bench. During confessions they placed the woman on Father's way so that he could touch her on his way out. True to their plan and prayer, as Father walked back to the podium he noticed her and laid hands on her. To the shock of all those present, the woman jumped to her feet and burst out in songs of praise. Every one acknowledged the action of God's power over evil. In the case of diviners the source of power is the spirits; either ancestral or other spirits with whom the diviner associates and works with.

From the researcher's observation, diviners seem to possess some heightened intuition. They are able to sense something that is about to happen. As already mentioned in chapter five, Syokwia one of the blind diviners visited by this researcher interrupted the interviews and claimed she had been shown that I belonged to a special vocation and that I was far from them. This inspiration was true regardless of its source. As a consecrated nun I have in a way defied culture and there is no doubt that my faith moves on a contrary motion to that of the diviner. Downey (1993: 555) points out that with mystics, there is the possibility in the contemplative experience of an immediate knowing of God in which the subject-object dichotomy disappears.

Diviners are hard nuts to crack when it comes to their faith. They are people with very firm stand when it comes to their traditional practices. Interviews and observation of all the diviners in the selected sample proved that they would not welcome any attempts to deviate them from their way. In fact some of them repeatedly mentioned that if they deviate from the instructions of their spiritual partners in the work, something serious would befall them. Despite their firm stand, they respect people of other faiths.

Diviners are to their adherents a source of social security. Through the witchcraft eradication rituals performed on witches and members of their families and clans, individual treatment against witchcraft and treatment of homesteads, those concerned acquired a feeling of security. By living according to the cultural beliefs and practices that were usually enhanced through the activities of the diviner such as, offering sacrifice to appease an offended spirit, people felt more secure, closer to their community and developed a higher sense of belonging. Viewed from a cultural stand point, those separated from this social reality were looked upon as betrayers by those living in it. That is why some Christians who belong to families with people that share in this view may find themselves hooked in with time.

Diviners have their culturally defined roles to play in the life of the community. Some of these culturally motivated roles relate to taboos, traditional oaths, belief in witchcraft and curses. All the four forces are believed to affect human life in one way or another hence the need for specialized form of healing. In the case of broken taboos, Freud says "the threat of punishment is superfluous because an inward certainty exists that violation will be followed by unbearable disaster... This results in compulsive acts which now must be done because they have acquired a compulsive character such as, penances and purifications" (2000: 47-50). According to the researcher, because of the deep rooted fear of the above forces, some Christians cooperated or were forced to the diviner for rituals. By these rituals, guilt is annulled and broken relationships are restored. The very pre-occupation of Christians with witchcraft beliefs and witchcraft eradication processes by the diviner affirms that the diviner is widely accepted in the community as having palatable solutions to their daily life turmoils. In this case, the diviner becomes a psychotherapist, a counselor and a ritualistic healer.

In line with the belief in diviners the researcher underlines belief as one vital element that influences people's behaviour a great deal. Belief must be preceded by knowledge of something as good or bad, acceptable or unacceptable in order for it to trigger a response. In the same way, because the Akamba believe that witchcraft, traditional oaths, broken taboos and curses are rooted in the culture and that a cultural diviner is the only one that can sort out such negative forces, so long as diviners exist, those who hold to this belief will always consult them.

Beyond the spiritual and social healing, diviners deal with crisis situations. Drawing from the common responses from the field, diviners are not consulted for any situation but as a final solution when all else has failed. They come in to determine who or what is causing the undesired situation. If the cause is the ancestors, the necessary steps are taken such as, holding a ritual dance *kilumi* in the name of the afflicted spirit, offering the required sacrifices and libations or buying the kind of cloth demanded for by the spirits. By this, the offended spirits are appeased as the victim is assured of a better future.

In relation to the healing practices of diviners, the researcher refutes claims that the Akamba diviners are pure herbalists. This notion is a recent innovation and a modern academic approach which does not reflect the reality on the ground. Instead, the typical Akamba diviners take their medicines through a ritual of seven counts during which words to commend the medicine to the influence of certain spirits are articulated. By this ritual, all poisonous elements are eliminated and the good medicine is empowered for healing purposes. Among the Akamba there is a very poisonous plant known as *Kilyambiti*. This plant is used by diviners for healing after the seven round rituals. Whatever is done to these plants is the prerogative of the diviner. This implies that many people who visit diviners do not know the secret behind the medicines they receive from them nor the kind of rituals undertaken before administration of these medicines. This means that diviners conceal a lot of secrets from their clients and no wonder some Christians seem to see nothing wrong with the diviners' therapies.

Drawing from the experience with diviners, the researcher describes them as, very welcoming people, empathetic, confident in their profession and very patient with their clients. As persons, they seem to share in some useful skills of dealing with people in a way that is human. Even though many of the Akamba diviners do not have much formal training, to a certain extent they act professionally. This manner of behaviour is a possible source of attraction to clients. In the view of the researcher, this kind of approach to clients reduces fear in new clients. It makes diviners more acceptable to the community.

The confession of some Catholic respondents that they had either personally been treated by diviners or their family members or their neighbours shows that some Christians found the diviner useful in one way or another. This conclusion is further propelled by confession of Christian respondents that many of them had been obliged by clan decisions to participate in witchcraft eradication oaths and rituals administered by the diviner. According to the victims, some of them had already undergone the Diocesan form of punishment for such offenses, some for a period of three months and others for one year. Although a good number dreaded the ritual, some felt it was useful in restoring harmony in the formerly disintegrated families.

From the ideas gathered from Christian respondents, the researcher concludes that lack of proper evangelization of new converts to Christianity, inadequate follow up of the baptized and influence of the diviner friendly Christians on fellow Christians are some of the contributing factors to Christian relapse to their traditional practices involving the diviner.

The Way forward

Since the first chapter of this piece of work, the main focus has been the question of Christian involvement with diviners. Since the problem of Christians yielding to their traditional beliefs and practices involving the diviner has been rampant in various parts of Machakos, the study proposes that the Church should seek to understand more deeply the appeal of the diviner among the Catholics and give it a biblical evaluation. It is the high time that the question of diviners was accorded closer attention by priests in particular and catechists with the objective of understanding the diviners' ministry so as to establish why Christians consult them. In order to achieve this end, some fundamental questions need to be answered in the light of the Gospel such as, why is it that some Christians result to the diviner and not to the Church in time of crisis? Should this enigma be viewed, as a mere manifestation of human weakness and sin or it bears sharper edges that point to deeper gaps and needs in the people that have not been adequately addressed by the Church?

During the field study, the researcher felt deep yearning among the people of the need to evaluate the current methods of evangelization for growth away from conflicting cultural practices to be achieved. Honest evaluation of the diviner within the context of the Akamba culture would enable agents of evangelization and the entire Christian community to answer with more confidence the questions; "what has gone wrong? Who has failed? What can be done?" This according to the researcher in agreement with the Christian respondents would facilitate deeper unity in faith among the Christians.

During this study, it was revealed that some catechists still applied methods that did not challenge the faith of the catechumens. Most commonly used approach was the memorization skill mostly favored by old catechists. It is the view of this researcher that if young initiates to the Christian faith are not finely introduced to the Christian doctrine, and well guided in their day to day life skills, this major short fall may create a gap that may be filled by culture based faith. A shift from the traditional method of cramming to reflection on the meaning and implications of the word of God in one's life should be adopted by all teachers of faith and not by catechists only. Young Christians

213

should be introduced to practical works of mercy such as visiting the sick and praying with them. By so doing, these young and energetic minds will be pre-occupied with the Christian culture, its beliefs and practices.

Training of evangelization ministers is highly recommended by this study. Training is recommended for its ability to equip agents of evangelization with the necessary content and skills for its dissemination. In this regard, the African Synod Fathers (1995:18) strongly recommended that all those engaged in evangelization, Bishops, Priests, religious, Catechists and Laity should be trained for evangelization. Their voices were echoed in the Lineamenta on the Word of God (2007:48) which presents this same challenge by asking the following fundamental questions: "Are future priests, consecrated persons and those responsible for various services in the community properly formed and periodically up-dated in the biblical aspects of their pastoral ministry? Are there ongoing programs of formation for the laity? In a particular way, these two questions call for proper planning in those parishes where training of agents of evangelization is not yet a priority. The Akamba diviners never made a prompt entry into their ministry. Instead, they undertook rigorous training during which skills and content proper to their ministry were imparted. Proper training of evangelizers is, key to the genuine understanding of Christian faith and its subsequent insertion into the cultural values.

Apart from training and implementing ongoing formation programs for the existing agents of evangelization it should be realized that those in the field are still inadequate. This short fall was strongly expressed by the Christian respondents who felt that the current number of priests was quite low as compared to the number of Christians under their pastoral care. Observation of the researcher was that with the exception of town parishes such as, Machakos Cathedral, the usual number of priests in each Parish was two. Presently, this count is overwhelmed by the high apostolic demands heightened by the growing numbers of Christians hence the need to consider the training of lay evangelizers. In relation to the need to increase on the number of agents of evangelization, this study recommends that, thorough scrutiny be made before one is accepted as an agent of evangelization and rigorous initiation programs put in place especially for new evangelizers. Another solution to this should be a prayer for the increase of vocations and for strengthening the priestly ministry in the Diocese through whom Christ continues to reach out to his people.

On evangelization, this study is concordant with Mutisya's recommendation that it be carried out by the local people. His view and the view of other respondents was that the local people understood their language better than foreign missionaries. In Kikamba, there are certain words that cannot adequately be translated into English. The choice of local people for evangelization is also based on the fact that they have been born and lived the culture to a larger extent. In this case, they are in a better position to challenge their fellows from within. The most popular Akamba diviners are those born and inculcated into the Akamba culture. Diviners succeeded in convincing their clients because they have a fine understanding of the people's cultural beliefs and practices. Having been socialized into the culture they are not only rhetorically sound but also have a command of symbols that accompany language hence the ability to attract clients.

The Catholic Church has since the Second Vatican Council sounded the urgent need for the Church in Africa to engage in a methodological approach to the Gospel that corresponds to the people's way of thinking taking into account their values, language, art and symbols. According to the Vatican II document; Nostra Aetates (in Shoter, 1987: 26), the Catholic Church rejects nothing of what is true and holy in non-Christian religions. In addition, Kariuki (in Shoter, 1987: 155) alludes that Africans have rich values which would be ennobled through dialogue with corresponding Gospel values. Owing to this urgent need expressed by the universal Church to plant into the people's lives the Gospel of Christ in a manner that appeals to them, the Catholic Church in Machakos is challenged to address the question of Christian involvement with diviners in the light of the Gospel where this can apply. The Church needs to evaluate her attitude towards diviners, who are viewed by the Akamba as traditional specialists providing them with the means to confront evil in the community. Chief J.Ngui (personal communication, March 6, 2008) an elderly Catholic believer had this to say "What is not harmful in the culture, what is positive and helpful to the people and that which does not conflict with the gospel values should be allowed in the Church" This government officer and a Christian was of the opinion that where the diviner was useful to the community in revealing evil doers the Church should allow it as a step towards inculturation. While this sounds quite sensible, this researcher is of the opinion that any meaningful inculturation must give room to experts to examine the content and to recommend to the Christian community the way forward. This should be done to eliminate the risk of syncretism. During the field study, a diviner reiterated that her ministry was equal to that of a priest since they both used the same type of plant (mutaa) in cleansing. If such instruments used in traditional religion are directly applied to Christianity without proper explanation it will draw many to think that the Church has no problem with traditional practices which may not be true. Great care has to be taken not to create an impression that the Church is in harmony with the idea of, and the practice of divination.

Pope Paul VI in one of his apostolic exhortations remarked "For the Church, evangelization means bringing the Good News into all the strata of humanity from within" (Evangelii Nuntiandi, 13). In their efforts to deepen the people's faith in Christ, agents of evangelization should ask themselves, "Supposing Christ was physically walking in the streets of our city, how possibly would he deal with the conflict in families and clans arising from the belief in witchcraft? How would he offload the burden of guilt from the victims of broken taboos? How would he deal with culprits whose socially destabilizing acts for example, theft cannot be proven by the court? How would he handle Christians who have undergone treatment with diviners? Since the word of God enters in a culture to purify it from within, solutions based on Jesus' words and deeds should be sought to the crucial situation of Christian attraction to diviners in the Diocese from within. When the love of Jesus became incarnate in the life of Zacchaeus, he became completely transformed. A man once egoistic and materialistic, when he came head on with Jesus, he immediately became aware of his shortcomings and turned his attention to the poor, a sign of repentance (Luke 19: 5-8). To heighten the people's experience of the salvific presence of Christ, every possibility has to be exploited to ensure that the message of Christ is presented to them in metaphors that they can hear, see, touch and comprehend.

As already noted elsewhere in this dissertation, the diviner diagnoses the cause or causes of a problem, cures different diseases and illnesses and, deals with the widespread problem of witchcraft among others. Kyule (Session paper, February, 2004) in his paper on inculturation expresses the need for the Church to understand the deep rooted fear among Africans that cannot be attributed to superstition but to the African world view that attributes illness to breaking of taboos, traditional oaths, offending God or spirits. In their approach to healing, diviners understand this variety of causes prompting them to put into consideration all these possible causes to human suffering. Diviners heal by leading people to acknowledge their evil deeds, by reconciling those in strained relationships, by giving herbs and rituals for psychological healing for example, placing a live chicken on some one's head to cure migraines. In addressing the problem of human suffering, the Church has to consider adopting an integral approach in order to win the confidence of her children. For example, if a man tormented by an evil spirit approached you, the parish priest for deliverance, how would you react? By immediate confrontation of evils that threaten human life, evangelizers place themselves on the seat of Jesus, the word incarnate.

Reflection on the question of the Church's response to bi-religious attitude among some of her members, led the researcher to conclude that preaching against diviners and punishing Christians who went to them was far from being enough. Instead, the Church has to invent practical ways of relieving people of both physical and spiritual atrocities, emanating from the cultural beliefs and practices. For instance, there seems to be a relationship between the Akamba attitude towards broken taboos, its effect on a victim's life and Paul's view of the Corinthian community. He remarks, "For if he does not recognize the meaning of the Lord's body when he eats the bread and drinks from the cup, he brings judgment on himself as he eats and drinks. That is why many of you are sick and weak, and several have died" (1Corinthians 11: 29-30). In this case, sin (thavu) of disrespect to the body and blood of Christ can result into physical suffering according to Paul. This can be equated to a daughter's sexual relationship with the father which is a taboo to the Akamba culture. When the Akamba use the term *thavu* in relation to such an act, it caries a heavier weight than it would when translated into the word sin in English. *Thavu* in its traditional usage calls for ritual cleansing by a diviner in order to restore the victims to a state of harmony with the community. To lift those Catholic Christians who hold on to this belief out of it, the Church must first of all seek to understand the concept of sin from the cultural perspective to be able to device a convincing approach of freeing victims of broken taboos from the diviner.

From the sociological point of view, we realize that diviners fulfill a vital need among the people. One of the key findings of this study was that diviners provide security to the people. When people, receive from the diviners medicine to protect themselves from witches, their business and homesteads, their fears are driven away. Fear is one of the strongest drives in a human being that can cause great havoc in one's life if not checked. The Akamba culture through the diviner endows the community with the means to counter this drive to those affected in order to ensure harmony in the community. The Church on her part and in the interest of the gospel should endevour to provide tangible security to her members by putting in place feasible tools towards this effort. To this direction, this study calls on the Church to consider benefiting her members through the professional services of counselors. These counselors should be individuals of fair understanding of the Akamba culture as well as the Church's doctrine. It is the belief of this researcher that these counselors through the virtues of listening, empathy, understanding and trust would be able to swim deep into the clients' fears and together find ways and means of eliminating them. Prayer over tormented Christians is necessary. Charismatic gifts that God has given to His Church should be put into proper use.

The study proposes that Christians be molded into the culture of having the Eucharist celebrated in their homes. It is inconceivable the amount of blessings Christ bestows in a home where he is allowed in. In the spirit of faith, Christians threatened by the fear of witchcraft instead of calling on the diviner to plant medicines around the homes should invite a Priest to celebrate the Holy Eucharist. In the document 'On the Sacrament of Redemption' (2004: 5) it is stated:

> In the most Holy Eucharist, the Mother Church with steadfast faith acknowledges the Sacrament of Redemption...celebrates it and reveres it in adoration, proclaiming the death of Christ Jesus and confessing his resurrection until he comes in glory to hand over as unconquered Lord and ruler, eternal Priest and King of the Universe, a kingdom of truth and life to the immense majesty of the Almighty Father.

At every Eucharistic celebration, Christians surrender all their cares and burdens to the Lord Jesus Christ who has already conquered the kingdom of evil.

As already noted the Akamba who consult diviners during difficult moments regardless of their faith, are in pursuit of healing of one kind or the other. The search for wholeness is one of the greatest pains of the human person. However, in the Eucharist Jesus draws us into a new bond of love which is established and accomplished through the sharing of his body and blood. Benedict XVI (2005: 20) remarks that the Eucharist draws us into Jesus' act of self oblation. By offering himself as the perfect Lamb at the altar, he becomes for all who trust in him a spring of healing water. As Christians receive Jesus in the Holy Eucharist, they come face to face with the perfect doctor and healer of all diseases and illnesses. This reality should therefore be continually preached to the Christian community in the simplest way possible in order to lead all to the understanding of this essential reality.

The use of sacramentals in the form of holy water, salt, pictures and articles such as, the Holy Rosary should be encouraged too. In their use, sacramentals are not to be taken as a simple replacement of the charmed rings or bungles from diviners. Rather, these holy objects are to be viewed as articles of faith that not only lead the faithful to a deeper expression of their faith but also deepen it in the course of directing one's spiritual hungers to the one and true God through prayer and devotion.

If the Catholic Church in Machakos Diocese is to maintain potent faith, Christians must be constantly reminded of the wonderful treasure at their disposal, Christ the Lord who is the way, the truth and the life" (John 14: 6). Ong'om (2007) narrated to the researcher of his encounter with a diviner in a study session who remarked "The spirit in which you believe is stronger than the spirit that guides a diviner, if only you Christians would realize it" God's supremacy over all existence is clearly articulated by Paul in his proclamation that, God created everything in heaven and on earth, the unseen things, including spiritual powers, lords, rulers and authorities (Colossi ans 1:16) It is therefore true that God's power to overcome all evil is unfailing since He is Creator of all. This reality should be rocked among the Christians through ongoing faith formation programs for all the baptized, each according to their level of growth in faith, strengthened focus on Small Christian Communities, consistent preparation for and administration of the sacraments especially the sacrament of reconciliation, days of recollection and retreats, counseling and spiritual direction, daily family prayer, forums for Christians to meet their pastors and other agents of evangelization for further guidance on their faith and life issues that may deter their progress in faith.

This study recommends common Bible study sessions facilitated by people with fair knowledge of the Bible. Common reflection on the word of God is a necessary step towards unveiling to the Christian community the mysteries of God, his plan and purpose for the humanity. An in-depth reflection is needed to make a distinction between everything in the Akamba belief system which can promote authentic Christian values and what stands against it. According to Benedict XVI, common reflection must underlie any pastoral activity (II Special Assembly for Africa, Lineamenta, 2006: 25). On the same breath, the XII ordinary General assembly on the Word of God (2007) lays great emphasis on the Word of God as the source of life and as a means of encountering the Lord in a personal way. Without full understanding of the person of Christ, Christianity will remain foreign to the very people that comprise it.

The study revealed the presence of some nominal Christians in the Diocese, a situation that may not entirely be blamed on them. In his study of the "primitive" societies, Emile Durkheim (1963: 26) remarks that collective habits in society acquire a permanent expression by being passed on from generation to the next. These according to him impel people to certain behaviors. Culture instills in individuals beliefs that may lead to certain practices that if not properly countered may leave one fully immersed in his/her traditional faith. In order for the Christians to be directed towards meaningful experience of Christian faith, there is need for clarification on those aspects in traditional culture that conflict with the Christian teaching. It is not enough to punish those who participate in activities of the diviner without proper explanation as to why such involvement is not compatible with Christianity.

In response to the above need, the study proposes dialogue between the Church, diviners and other traditional worshipers. Diviners feel that Christians are prejudiced against them. Mutio told the researcher that Christians called them devilish, yet in her long service as a diviner she had never seen the devil. This researcher reiterates that unless there is meaningful communication between the traditional and Christian models of faith, each will continue to be strange to the other. At the same time, Christianity will remain foreign to those who feel that it does not address their needs as effectively as their culture does. Through dialogue the Church may have the opportunity to understand the phenomena of evil from a cultural point of view better than before leading to easier penetration of the Christian message into the people's situations.

Kyule explaining the current bi-religious situation among the Akamba

223

(Session paper, February 2004), dates the problem back to the period of transformation from ancestral worship to Christianity. He states that, during this period, many questions were left unanswered. This study concurs with his firm recommendations that the Church makes an effort to track down the problem from its roots and to try to understand the African world view in order to comprehend why people revert to diviners in time of crisis. The experience of the researcher with diviners was that, when asked why they did most of the things during divination sessions, the most common response was "that is the way it should be" This response was an indication that traditional practices were inherited from one generation to the other. For this reason, African traditional religious beliefs and practices should be taught at all levels of education including seminaries. Professionals should spearhead the formulation and introduction of a curriculum that takes into account the African world view. The topic on witchcraft which in most cases becomes the cause of Christian interaction with diviners should be taught by people that are well informed of their culture and Christian doctrine as well.

The study found out that diviners are very strong in their traditional faith and that they treated it as an infringement of their right to the freedom of worship if Christians attempted to evangelize them. Through this study, it became very clear that diviners understood too well their identity as cultural specialists and the mandate to fulfill the mission entrusted to them by their ancestors. N. Kaleli (personal communication, March 8, 2008) asserted:

> I am a priest at the level of the Father in-charge of this parish; I have a special role to play just as much as he has. To stop me from my ministry is an offense and lack of respect to the one who commissioned me and a disadvantage my clients.

This bold stand is a big challenge to the Church. With this in mind, the researcher commends that commitment to one's faith forms one of the basic contents for on-going formation programs. This sense of commitment to one's faith must be inculcated into the young in Sunday schools, during catechetical classes and after baptism. It is the duty of the evangelization team to find relevant instructional materials particularly visual aids because what a child sees is retained in the memory higher than what has been verbalized. During homilies and other faith formation opportunities, this bold faith of diviners should challenge the Christian community to take a firm stand and responsibility over their Christian faith, freely chosen.

As the Church makes an effort to contain her members within the boundaries of sincere and honest faith, members must be made to realize that the work of evangelization is the challenge of the whole Christian community. This means that all the baptized have the potential to lead one another to the fullest experience of the char isms and gifts that the Holy Spirit endows to the Church. The study strongly recommends that the Catholic Christians see themselves as ambassadors and participants in the saving ministry of Christ. Once each is able to assume her/his then what Gehman envisages as impossible will be history. He warns that, should one remove the diviner or the medicine man/woman from the Akamba, one would need to replace him/her with another person who would fulfill a similar role (2002: 86). The idea of replacement may be a difficult and challenging because humans can be replaced externally but never internally. However, agents of evangelization should ask themselves the following fundamental questions;

  1. Do Christians who come to me in search of help leave my presence

better or worse than they came?

2. How do I handle Christians who approach me for any form of healing?

3. What is my attitude towards those suspected of having involvements with diviners?

All in all, Christians must arise to the voice of the Holy Spirit and demonstrate in words and actions their truest faith in Christ.

Although agents of evangelization experience innumerable challenges in their pastoral activities, this study proposes that these be faced as stepping stones towards deeper commitment to the course of evangelization. Over and above all ways used to evangelize the people, the most noticeable means among them should be Christian witness. During the field study it surfaced that some of the leaders who were also agents of evangelization were among those consulting diviners. In this case, although theoretically they were opposed to the works of diviners, practically they approved of it. To avoid misleading acts, agents of evangelization should be cautious in all they do and say so that their lives become living witness of true Christian faith. Syokwia one of the diviners interviewed during the study discarded a rosary given to her by a priest to avoid being mistaken for a Christian by her clients. Christian evangelizers should learn from diviners the exercise of the virtue of honest in terms of faith identity. If anything, the Akamba diviners are proud of their traditional faith and will scoff at any one who attempts to preach to them.

From reading, observation and listening to different people during the field study, the researcher found it unhealthy for Christians to involved themselves with diviners who drew from the abundance of a cultural heritage that by nature is not motivated by the same Gospel values that define Christianity. Even if these were to be traced, Christianity still maintains a unique phenomenon that is foreign to this culture. Without any bias, it is worth articulating that although from the cultural point of view the diviner stands out as the only expert in those culturally rooted ailments that are considered detrimental to the health of individuals and community. Christians, due to the very nature of their faith stand on two standards if they consult a diviner. This assertion is based on the observations that:

1. The source of the diviner's power is ambiguous. From their own confession, all the diviners interacted with during the study attributed their success to the intervention of some spiritual forces that did not allow them to commune with the Church. One of the diviners, Mutio firmly asserted told this researcher that in their ministry they did not know Jesus and that he featured nowhere among us. From this statement we can deduce that it is not the spirit of Jesus at work in the diviner since diviners work with spirits familiar to them. At least three of the diviners interviewed narrated to the researcher about their efforts to join the Church and the subsequent failure of their efforts due to visible blocks as already mentioned in chapter five. Jesus declares about the nature of His Spirit:

   However, when the Spirit comes, who reveals the truth about God; he will lead you into all truth. He will not speak of his own authority, but he will speak of what he hears and will tell you of things to come. He will give me glory because he will take what I say and give it to you. All that the Father has is mine; that is why I said that the Spirit will take what I give him and tell it to you (John 16: 13-15).

2. Diviners believe in the presence of different spirits and from time to time offer sacrifices to them, to appease and placate them in search of their favours. This belief is manifested in the storage of a number of drums, with each drum dedicated to a particular spirit. The most evil spirit known to the Akamba is *Kathambi*. This spirit possesses people mostly during the *kilumi* dances and must therefore be placated from time to time in order to keep it silent and calm. On the other hand Christianity teaches that all honor, worship and adoration must be directed to the one and true God Creator of all that exists. Jesus told Satan, "The Scripture says, 'worship the Lord your God and serve only him! (Luke 4: 8, cf. Dt. 6:13). Offering of sacrifice whether to ancestral spirits or other spirits may be viewed as a way of paying homage to them which is not in harmony with the Christian invitation to pay homage to God alone. Secondly, when an animal sacrifice is made for example, in the case of a sick person, the cultural understanding is that, the animal only stands in the gap, but the actual sacrifice to whichever spirit that demands it, is the sick person. For Christians, Christ by his death on the cross has offered one single sacrifice once and for all. This means that no sacrifice other than of Christ can please God. Diviners believe in prayer through the ancestors as the top means through which human afflictions are tackled and healing effected.

3. As already noted earlier, some diviners enter into a blood covenant with clients before a divination session. This is something similar to a cultist act. Further more, the researcher learned from the respondents that whenever the diviner makes incisions on a client's body usually there is bleeding. This blood is an offering to the spirits. Even without the knowledge of the person, he/she is slowly being dedicated to the spirits. Diviners too made it clear to the researcher that spirits like blood quite a lot. This explains why

at every divination session there is always the prescription of a goat for sacrifice except in very rare cases.

4. When Christians involve themselves with diviners no matter how much they benefit from this relationship they jeopardize their faith. The faith of a Christian is rooted in the death and resurrection of Jesus Christ. In plain terms, there is no way a Christian whose faith oscillates between faith in Jesus and faith in the diviner can claim a personal knowledge of the real nature and the person of Jesus. It is the belief of this researcher that when a person is torn between two opposing forces, one is sure to win and the other to loose the battle. Jesus himself understood it well when he said "No one can be a slave of two masters; he will hate one and love the other; he will be loyal to one and despise the other" (Matthew 6: 24). When Christians are diviner friendly they risk losing their faith in God altogether hence the need for them to be helped to understand their Christian identity and to maintain their faith boundaries.

During the field study it came to the awareness of the researcher that some chiefs collaborated with the community in search of culprits through diviners as the last option. In this connection the study recommends that the Church moves into such situations to provide proper direction.

Finally the study reiterates that although the diviner has been viewed as an opposer of Christian faith, there are certain values in them that could enrich Christianity. Some of them are:

- Clear understanding of their call- Diviners are very clear about their call to divination and the one behind it. They have unwavering respect and reverence of the spirits with whom they work. Christians ought to understand that to become a Christian is a divine call

- High sense of commitment to duty- Observations of the researcher were that diviners spend the better part of their day at home waiting for clients. Their sense of commitment was also noted in the full attention they accorded their clients. Christians and especially priests should learn from the patience of diviners with their clients. It is better to solve the problem of one client satisfactorily than to have ten clients who go home dissatisfied.

- Clear vision of mission- Diviners are very clear about their vision and mission. They share a common belief that they have been called to a special mission among the people; to diagnose, to heal and to alleviate suffering in the society. If Christians who visited diviners were as clear as diviners about their mission to live according to the gospel demands and to spread it to others, Christian faith would be stronger in the Diocese.

- Knowledge of their traditions and practices- To become a diviner one important requirement is to have clear knowledge of the community's' traditional beliefs and practices. Christianity has its traditional beliefs, values and practices that call for proper initiation. Like the diviners, Christians should strive to respect and to safeguard their own values and to live them faithfully.

- Open hearted- Christians should learn from the open hearted of the diviner. They do not segregate clients. Instead they serve all those who come to them indiscriminately.

The above values in the Akamba culture, given a Christian face would lead to deeper acceptance of Christian faith while at the same time checking Christian dualism.

Conclusion

Society survives through the generous contribution of its members in terms of spiritual and material benefits. On their part, humans benefit from society in its provision of identity, personality and security among others. As established by this study, Africans find in the diviner a definition of their culture through his use of different traditional tools such as the horn of a duiker, a rubbing stick or rubbing board among the Yaka people of Zaire (Rene Devisch, in Peek, 1991: 113). Among the Agikuyu, traditional diviners have *rogambi* as their preferred tool (Kenyatta, 1978: 192). The diviner among the Akamba gives identity to the community as a cultural specialist. In this case they are revered as cultural authorities. Crollins (in Walligo et al 1986: 53) states that the world acquires its own identity by the self realization of the human person. He opines that by developing themselves, people acquire perfection by means of their activity in the external world. In the traditional Akamba community, it was the diviner to provide direction and guidance in order for one to achieve this development.

In view of the different roles performed by diviners, their clients experience consolation and acquire a sense of security through the fulfillment of their needs. As a traditional specialist, the African diviner plays a key role in maintaining community harmony which extends to the spiritual world.

From the study, we have been able to establish that the Akamba diviners look to the ancestral spirits for their spiritual nourishment. It is from these same ancestral spirits that diviners inherit powers to accomplish their designated roles in the community. The argument by Kyule (Session paper, 2006) that Christianity has failed to shake off diviners because of their inherited powers is in agreement with the findings of this study. Mbiti (1992, 171) presents the same observation that in their profession, diviners also deal with the living-dead and spirits. The practice of inheritance in cultures is what facilitates continuity of what a given group of people hold dear to them.

This study established that the question of adherence to diviners was not confined to a particular continent, religion or ethnic community, but that it was a universal reality in the human society. For example, Freud (1963: 81-82) observes that the problem of taboo existed since the beginning in primitive societies including Rome. Taboos according to him are restrictions connected to the strongest desires of the human person and best manifested through incest. This explains the need for cleansing rituals to erase guilt from a victim's life performed by different African communities including the Akamba.

Having established the fact that diviners in Africa do not just exist in the mind but in reality, this study realizes the need for the Catholic Church in Africa and especially in Machakos Diocese where it became clear that some of her members were involved with diviners, to rise up to this reality and to come up with a solution to it. The greatest challenge is to make an effort to discover the underlying cause of this bi-religious reality. The second challenge is for the Church to design practical ways and means of filling in the felt lacuna in these Christians. If Christianity is to find a home in the African Christians, this study reiterates that it must provide personality, identity and security which are the three most important benefits that individuals derive from their cultures. The Church needs to create favorable conditions that promote growth in faith among her members.

The practice of divination is as old as human cultures. The culture of a people manifests itself in vertical and horizontal movements. In this sense, the question of Christian attraction to diviners is indirectly a question of cultural loyalty. The view of the diviner as a relevant person in the contemporary Christian community, has its basis in the the people's world view. This study therefore concludes by urging for a pragmatic approach to the current Church's enigma. The most viable option for the growth and benefit of Christian faith is for the agents of evangelization to exert their energy to the course of study of their people's world view. The world view of a people articulates their culture. Culture is hereby understood as the sum total of all that people do, their ideas, manner of expressing emotions, beliefs and practices, language, leisure activities, likes and dislikes, behavior patterns, symbols, art including colours and shapes, tools, economic and spiritual orientations. To comprehend the behaviour of any cultural group, it warrants a thorough study of its world view. This approach is not only necessary but vital as it prepares the ground for an interpretation of the group's beliefs and practices in a manner that is free of bias. Such a step will form the basis for the identification of authentic African values into which the Christian message can genuinely and permanently be incarnated.

REFERENCES

Aidan, N. (1991). *The shape of Catholic Theology*. Minnesota: The order of St. Benedict, Inc.

Akiiki, B. (1982). *Religion in Bunyoro*. Nairobi: Kenya Literature Bureau.

Baur, J. (1990). *The Catholic Church in Kenya*. Nairobi: Paulines publications.

Berger, P.(1967). *Elements of a Sociological Theory of Religion*. N. Y: Dobleday & Company Inc.

Bidney, D. (1996). *Theoretical Anthropology*: Second Edition. New Jersey: Transaction Publishers.

Benedict XVI (2005). God is Love. Vaticana: Libreria Editrice.

_____ (2007). *The Sacrament of Charity: Post synodal Apostolic Exhortation*.
   Vaticana: Libreria Editrice.

Bruno, N. (1999). *Karimojong Traditional Religion*. Kampala: Componi Missionaries.

Crawford, J. (1963). *Witchcraft and Sorcery in Rhodesia*. London: Oxford University Press.

Emile D. (1963). *Major Contributions to Social Science Series*. N.Y: Thomas
    Y. Crowell Company, Inc.

Freud, S. (2000). *Totem and Taboo*. N.Y: Prometheus Books.

Fedders, A. et al (1994). *People's and Cultures of Kenya*. Nairobi: Trans
    Africa

Gehman, R. (1989). *African Traditional Religion in Biblical perspective*.
    Nairobi: East African Educational Publishers.

Good News Bible (1979). New York: American Bible Society.

Guardini, R. (1963). *Prayer and practice*. New York: A Division of
    Doubleday & Company, Inc.

Idowu, B. (1973). *The African Traditional religion.: A definition*. London:
    SCM press.

Isaac D. (1990). *The African Religion and Philosophy.* Nairobi: Mailu
    Publishing House.

Jomo K. (1978). *Facing Mount Kenya*. Nairobi: Kenway Publications.

Kirwen M. (2005). *African Cultural Knowledge: Themes and embedded
beliefs.*_Nairobi: MIAS BOOKS.

235

Kimilu, D.N. (1962). *Mukamba wawo*. Nairobi: Kenya Literature Bureau.

Knight, K. (2003) *The Catholic encyclopedia: Volume X*, Online Edition.

http://www.newadvent.org/cathen/10735a.htm.

Keek, E (1994). *The New interpreter's Bible*; Vol II. Nashville: Abindon
    Press.

Lindblom, G.n (1920). *The Akamba in British East Africa*. New York: Negroe

    University's press.

Majawa, C. (2005). *Integrated Approach to African Christian Theology of
    Inculturation. Nairobi.* The Catholic University of Eastern Africa.Book
    Distributors.

Magesa, L. (1997). *African Religion: The Moral Traditions of Abundant Life.*
    Nairobi: Paulines Publications Africa.

_____ (1998). *African Religion: The moral Traditions of Abundant life_*
_____Nairobi: Pauline Publications.

Mugambi, J.N.K. (1997). *The African Heritage and contemporary
    Christianity*, Nairobi: Longman Kenya Ltd.

Mugambi, J. and Kirima, N. (1976). *The African Religious Heritage.*
        Nairobi: Oxford University Press.

Mutiso, J. (1984). *The Eucharist and the Family-in an African setting,*
        AMECEA Documentation Service.

Morris, M. (1960). *Curing ritual: A causal and motivational*
        analysis in the realm of the Extra-Human: Ideas and Actions, Mouton:
The Hague.

Mbiti, J. (1992). *Introduction to African Religion: Second Edition.* Nairobi:
East African Educational Publishers.

Mbiti, J. (1995). *African Religions and Philosophy.* Nairobi: Heinneman
        Educational Books.

Mbula, J. (1982). *Our Religious Heritage.* Hong Kong: Thomas Nelson and
        sons.

Musembi, M. (1999). *The Akamba Religious view of the Human person.*
        Unpublished work, Nairobi.

Muthiani, J. (1973). *Akamba from within,* N.Y: Exposition Press.

Ndeti, J. (1972). *The Akamba Mirror.* Kijabe: Kesho Publications.

Ngong, T. (2004). *I Am because we provide.* Tigania: St. John of God Catholic

Hospital.

Ogburn, W. (1964). *Sociology*. N.Y: The Florida State University.

Okoti. B. (1971). *Religion of Central Luo.* Nairobi: East African Literature
Bureau.

Onwubiko, O. (2001). The *Church in Mission in the Light of Ecclesia in
Africa*.
Nairobi: St. Paul publications.

Underhill, E. (1961). *Mysticism: A study in the Nature of Man's spiritual
Consciousness*. New York: Dutton,

Parrinder, G. (1962). *African Traditional Religion.* London: S.P.C.K.

Patton, M. (1990). *Qualitative evaluation and Research methods.* Newbury
Park, California: SAGE Publications, Inc.

Peek, P. (1991). *African Divination systems*. Bloomington: Indiana University
Press.

Penwill D.J. (1986). *Kamba Customary Law*. Nairobi: Kenya Literature
Bureau

Pritchard, E. (1977). *Witchcraft, oracles and Magic among the Azande*.
London: Oxford University Press.

Shorter, A. (1985). *Jesus and the Witch-doctor*. London: Orbis Books.

Tempels, P. (1969). *Bantu Philosophy* Paris: Presence African.

Turner, V. W (1967). *The Ritual Process, structure and anti-structure.* New
     York: Aldine Publishing Company

Unger, M. F. (1972). *Demons in the world today*. Wheaton: Scripture Press.

Walligo, J.M.et al (1986). *Inculturation: Its Meaning and Urgency*. Nairobi:
St. Paul
     Communications

Wilkermann, D. (2004). *The Old Testament Philosophy and Culture*.
     Birmingham: Rose Publications.

Zahan, D. (1979). *The Religion, Spirituality, and Thought of Traditional
Africa.*
     Chicago: The University of Chicago Press.

Church Documents

Abbot, W.W (1966).*Gaudium et Spes" art. 3 in the Documents of Vatican II.*
     London: Geoffrey Chapman.

Benedict XVI (2005). *God is love: Encyclical letter Deus Caritas Est.*
     Nairobi: Pailines publications

Congregation for Divine Worship and Discipline of the Church (2004). *The Sacrament of Redemption: Instruction on Certain Matters to Be Observed or to Be avoided Regarding the Most Holy Eucharist.* Nairobi: St. Paul Communications.

II Special Assembly fro Africa (2006). *The Church in Africa in Service to Reconciliation, Justice and Peace: Lineamenta.* Nairobi: St. Paul Communications

XII Ordinary General Assembly (2007). *The Word of God In the Life And Mission Of The Church: Lineamenta.* Nairobi: St. Paul Communications

The Kenya Catholic Secretariat (2006).

The Catechism of the Catholic Church (1995). Nairobi: Paulines Publications, Nos. 499-500.

The African Synod (1994). *Pope's opening homely message of the synod message of the AMECEA and IMBISA.* Nairobi: Paulines publications

Machakos Diocese, Episcopal ordination, June, 2003

Journals

.Osunwole S. (1991). *Journal of Religious Studies.* Ibadan: xx111/1-2, June &

December

Unpublished material

Abimbola, W. (1976). *Ifa divination poems as sources for historical evidence.*
Lagos, notes and records.

Citizen paper, December 25, 2005, vol.9, number 5

Locheng, C. (2007). *Class Notes.*

Kasomo, D. (2000). *The Belief in mystical powers and its effects on lives of*
Akamba Catholics of Tawa Parish in Machakos Diocese, MA thesis,
CUEA,
Kenya.

_____(2003). *The Nature, Causes and participation in Traditional*
Oathing; The Case of the Akamba of Mwala, Machakos; Ph.D dissertation,
CUEA, Kenya.

Kaheeru, B. (1990). *Kiga Traditional Practices of Medicine and Healing in*
the Light of Christ's healing ministry in Luke, MA thesis, CUEA,
Kenya.

Kyule J. Session Paper, February, 2004

Kyule J. Session Paper, February, 2006

Magesa, L. (2006). *Pastoral response to witchcraft*; A seminar paper, 6th February, 2006, Tangaza College

Munuve, M. (2001). *The phenomenon of Masya/Ngata ritual as a witchcraft eradicator and deterrent among the Akamba*, MA thesis, Mary knoll School of Theology, U.S.A.

Ngundo, B.. (1999). *Impact of the belief in witchcraft on Christianity. Case of Muthetheni Christians, Machakos*. BA Project, CUEA, Kenya.

_____(2001). *An Investigation into the Kamba Traditional ways of Healing: Implications for Evangelization in Machakos Diocese*. MA Thesis, CUEA, Kenya.

Mwendwa, F. (1990*). Christ the Healer with reference to the Traditional Healing practices of the Akamba of Eastern Kenya*, MA thesis; CUEA, Kenya.

Sse gawa (2004). *Sickness among the Baganda of Uganda; A Pastoral care of the Sick.*. MA thesis, CUEA, Kenya.

Urbanus K. (2000). *Machakos Catholic Diocese, Pastoral letter to Priests*, 29th August.

242

Printed by
Schaltungsdienst Lange o.H.G., Berlin